INTRODUCING
ISSUES WITH
OPPOSING
VIEWPOINTS®

School Shootings

Lisa Idzikowski, Book Editor

GREENHAVEN
PUBLISHING

Published in 2020 by Greenhaven Publishing, LLC
353 3rd Avenue, Suite 255, New York, NY 10010

Copyright © 2020 by Greenhaven Publishing, LLC

First Edition

Library of Congress Cataloging-in-Publication Data

Names: Idzikowski, Lisa, editor.
Title: School shootings / Lisa Idzikowski, Book Editor.
Description: First edition. | New York : Greenhaven Publishing, 2020. |
  Series: Introducing issues with opposing viewpoints | Includes
  bibliographical references and index. | Audience: Grade 7-12.
Identifiers: LCCN 2018053312| ISBN 9781534505728 (library bound) | ISBN
  9781534505735 (pbk.)
Subjects: LCSH: School shootings—United States—Prevention—Juvenile
  literature. | Gun control—United States—Juvenile literature. |
  Schools—Safety measures—United States—Juvenile literature.
Classification: LCC LB3013.32 .S3473 2020 | DDC 371.7/82—dc23
LC record available at https://lccn.loc.gov/2018053312

Manufactured in the United States of America

Website: http://greenhavenpublishing.com

Contents

Foreword

Indulging in a wide spectrum of ideas, beliefs, and perspectives is a critical cornerstone of democracy. After all, it is often debates over differences of opinion, such as whether to legalize abortion, how to treat prisoners, or when to enact the death penalty, that shape our society and drive it forward. Such diversity of thought is frequently regarded as the hallmark of a healthy and civilized culture. As the Reverend Clifford Schutjer of the First Congregational Church in Mansfield, Ohio, declared in a 2001 sermon, "Surrounding oneself with only like-minded people, restricting what we listen to or read only to what we find agreeable is irresponsible. Refusing to entertain doubts once we make up our minds is a subtle but deadly form of arrogance." With this advice in mind, Introducing Issues with Opposing Viewpoints books aim to open readers' minds to the critically divergent views that comprise our world's most important debates.

Introducing Issues with Opposing Viewpoints simplifies for students the enormous and often overwhelming mass of material now available via print and electronic media. Collected in every volume is an array of opinions that captures the essence of a particular controversy or topic. Introducing Issues with Opposing Viewpoints books embody the spirit of nineteenth-century journalist Charles A. Dana's axiom: "Fight for your opinions, but do not believe that they contain the whole truth, or the only truth." Absorbing such contrasting opinions teaches students to analyze the strength of an argument and compare it to its opposition. From this process readers can inform and strengthen their own opinions, or be exposed to new information that will change their minds. Introducing Issues with Opposing Viewpoints is a mosaic of different voices. The authors are statesmen, pundits, academics, journalists, corporations, and ordinary people who have felt compelled to share their experiences and ideas in a public forum. Their words have been collected from newspapers, journals, books, speeches, interviews, and the internet, the fastest growing body of opinionated material in the world.

Introducing Issues with Opposing Viewpoints shares many of the well-known features of its critically acclaimed parent series, Opposing

Viewpoints. The articles allow readers to absorb and compare divergent perspectives. Active reading questions preface each viewpoint, requiring the student to approach the material thoughtfully and carefully. Photographs, charts, and graphs supplement each article. A thorough introduction provides readers with crucial background on an issue. An annotated bibliography points the reader toward articles, books, and websites that contain additional information on the topic. An appendix of organizations to contact contains a wide variety of charities, nonprofit organizations, political groups, and private enterprises that each hold a position on the issue at hand. Finally, a comprehensive index allows readers to locate content quickly and efficiently.

Introducing Issues with Opposing Viewpoints is also significantly different from Opposing Viewpoints. As the series title implies, its presentation will help introduce students to the concept of opposing viewpoints and learn to use this material to aid in critical writing and debate. The series' four-color, accessible format makes the books attractive and inviting to readers of all levels. In addition, each viewpoint has been carefully edited to maximize a reader's understanding of the content. Short but thorough viewpoints capture the essence of an argument. A substantial, thought-provoking essay question placed at the end of each viewpoint asks the student to further investigate the issues raised in the viewpoint, compare and contrast two authors' arguments, or consider how one might go about forming an opinion on the topic at hand. Each viewpoint contains sidebars that include at-a-glance information and handy statistics. A Facts About section located in the back of the book further supplies students with relevant facts and figures.

Following in the tradition of the Opposing Viewpoints series, Greenhaven Publishing continues to provide readers with invaluable exposure to the controversial issues that shape our world. As John Stuart Mill once wrote: "The only way in which a human being can make some approach to knowing the whole of a subject is by hearing what can be said about it by persons of every variety of opinion and studying all modes in which it can be looked at by every character of mind. No wise man ever acquired his wisdom in any mode but this." It is to this principle that Introducing Issues with Opposing Viewpoints books are dedicated.

Introduction

"It's not going to be talk like it has been in the past. It's been going on too long. Too many instances, and we're going to get it done…We're going to be very strong on background checks…We're going to go strong on age of purchase and the mental aspect.

—President Donald Trump on stopping gun violence, February 2018.

"We as a country failed our children. I can't get on a plane with a bottle of water. But some animal can walk into a school and kill our children…how many schools, how many children have to get shot? It stops here…I'm not going to sleep until it gets stopped.

—Andrew Pollack, father of Parkland High School shooting victim

Another school shooting has occurred." These words strike terror in the hearts of people everywhere. Is this phenomenon on the rise? Is everyone carrying a gun? Is anywhere safe? It may feel that school shootings are happening all the time. In truth they are not. Although multiple victim shootings are up, according to James Allan Fox, a criminologist at Northwestern University, schools are safer than they were in the 1990's, when there were more school shootings. The difference, Fox says, is the reporting style of the media. The twenty-four-hour news cycle keeps the coverage of school shootings front and center. Recordings of gunfire play over and over and over again. Listeners can hardly catch a breath. School shootings must be increasing, they reason.

School shootings fall into several categories. Rampage school shootings occur when no single or specific individual is targeted by the shooter. Mass school shootings happen when four or more victims are killed by a firearm at school. Multiple-victim school shootings represent events where there are four or more victims of firearms, two of whom die. Neither of these include the shooter in the victim count.

Although research shows that children are safer than at times in the past, people are worried more than ever. According to a 2018 poll conducted by the Pew Research Center, 64 percent of teen girls and 51 percent of teen boys are worried that a shooting may happen at their school. Their parents share the same concerns, with 63 percent saying they are somewhat worried about it happening. Can anything be done? Many teens believe that helping people with mental illness, including not letting those individuals obtain guns, would go a long way towards preventing school shootings. Some also want metal detectors installed in schools, and assault weapons banned. Some even favor arming teachers.

Not surprisingly, there is some agreement among adults, but there are also sharp differences. Many adults favor help for those with mental illness and agree with the potential banning of assault type weapons. But in other ways to prevent school shootings and mass shootings there is much disagreement. Most of it centers around the issue of gun control. There are proponents who favor gun control. They argue that guns increase violence, and without guns, incidents of killing would decrease. Some studies show they may be right. But not all studies agree. Opponents fight for their right to own weapons and want less gun control. They cite the Second Amendment to the US Constitution as a reason for their right to keep and bear arms.

Politicians, powerful groups and organizations, and individuals take both sides of the issue. The National Rifle Association (NRA) is a powerful lobbying group. They want lawmakers and the public to see the gun control issue their way. The NRA is convinced that most everyone should have a gun. Many American adults agree as about four-in-ten live in households that contain at least one gun. Americans own guns for different reasons—67 percent for protection, and 38 percent for hunting. Another idea pushed by gun proponents is the arming of classroom teachers. President Trump has suggested that highly trained individuals, including teachers, administrators, and security officials, should be armed in their schools and classrooms. Do people agree with the president? Some do. Almost three-quarters of Republican men think it's a good idea.

On the flip side, more than half of US adults don't want to see armed teachers in the classroom. 86 percent of women who identify as Democrat are against teachers packing heat. The American Federation of Teachers and the National Educational Association are in total agreement. Their presidents have issued a joint statement stating that "Guns have no place in our schools. Period. We must do everything we can to reduce the possibility of any gunfire in schools, and concentrate on ways to keep all guns off school property and ensure the safety of children and school employees. Lawmakers at every level of government should dismiss this dangerous idea and instead focus on measures that will create the safe and supportive learning environments our children deserve."

One thing is for certain: Everyone wants to end school shootings. And many knowledgeable individuals and organized groups are trying to do what they can to prevent this horrible form of violence. The current debate that surrounds the issue of school shootings is explored through diverse perspectives in *Introducing Issues with Opposing Viewpoints: School Shootings*, and sheds light on this divisive and ongoing contemporary issue.

Chapter 1

Are School Shootings an Epidemic?

After the tragedy at Marjory Stoneman Douglas High School in Parkland, Florida, Americans wondered if school shootings were the new normal.

It Only Seems Like School Shootings Are Increasing

Martin Kaste

"Schools are safer today than they had been in previous decades."

In the following viewpoint, Martin Kaste argues that the public perception that schools have become more dangerous than in previous decades is not based in fact. The author provides evidence from statistical studies that prove the incidence of school violence has decreased. His report claims that social media and the news cycle are giving a false sense of increased occurrence of school gun violence. As a correspondent for NPR, Martin Kaste covers stories about law enforcement, privacy issues, and world events.

AS YOU READ, CONSIDER THE FOLLOWING QUESTIONS:

1. According to the viewpoint, what is true about the incidence of school shootings?
2. As reported by the author, what is the best way to prevent school shootings?
3. What makes school shootings seem more of a threat as stated in the viewpoint?

The Parkland shooting last month has energized student activists, who are angry and frustrated over gun violence. But it's also contributed to the impression that school shootings are a growing epidemic in America.

In truth, they're not.

"Schools are safer today than they had been in previous decades," says James Alan Fox, a professor of criminology at Northeastern University who has studied the phenomenon of mass murder since the 1980s.

Fox and doctoral student Emma Fridel crunched the numbers, and the results should come as a relief to parents.

First, while multiple-victim shootings in general are on the rise, that's not the case in schools. There's an average of about one a year —in a country with more than 100,000 schools.

"There were more back in the '90s than in recent years," says Fox. "For example, in one school year—1997-98—there were four multiple-victim shootings in schools."

Second, the overall number of gunshot victims at schools is also down. According to Fox's numbers, back in the 1992-93 school year, about 0.55 students per million were shot and killed; in 2014-15, that rate was closer to 0.15 per million.

"The difference is the impression, the perception that people have," Fox says—and he traces that to cable news and social media. "Today we have cell phone recordings of gunfire that play over and over and over again. So it's that the impression is very different. That's why people think things are a lot worse now, but the statistics say otherwise."

Other experts agree. Garen Wintemute is an emergency room physician who leads a prominent gun violence research program at the University of California, Davis. He says school shootings, specifically, are not epidemic.

"Schools are just about the safest place in the world for kids to be," Wintemute says. "Although each one of them is horrific and rivets the entire nation for a period of time, mass shootings at schools are really very uncommon, and they are not increasing in frequency. What's changed is how aware we are of them."

Media coverage may be driving our perception that schools are less safe than they reallly are.

But Wintemute believes mass shootings—whether in schools or elsewhere—are increasing social pressure to address the far more common threat of small-scale shootings, which mostly happen in private.

"For school-age kids, the kind of shooting we most need to worry about is the kind of shooting that occurs off the school grounds," Wintemute says. "The best way to prevent school shootings is to prevent shootings in general."

He endorses broader gun safety measures, such as "red flag" laws, which give authorities the ability to remove firearms temporarily from people deemed to be threatening violence to themselves or others.

Wintemute and Fox say that by focusing so narrowly on school shootings, we run the risk of turning schools into fortresses. Fox says, given the statistics, it's misguided to put kids through metal detectors and active shooter drills, and he doesn't like the new calls for armed teachers.

"Most adults wouldn't want their workplaces to look like what some of the schools are looking like, now," Fox says.

But the perception of danger puts school administrators in a difficult position.

Marysville Pilchuck High School, about an hour north of Seattle, has experienced the tragedy of a shooting, and the statistical rarity is no comfort.

On Oct. 24, 2014, a freshman shot five other students in the cafeteria, killing four, before killing himself. Ever since, administrators have struggled to restore the students' sense of safety.

"Probably, every day it pops into your head at one time or another," says acting district superintendent Jason Thompson. "You think, 'Okay, we've had our shooting,' right? It's human to think that way. But I think a lot of times for me, it's like, 'This could happen again.'"

For the last three years, the district has wrestled with how to make schools safer, without going overboard. Local voters defeated a bond levy which would have remodeled the open-style campus into a more secure, single-entrance configuration. So the school remains very open. There's a new security camera, a security guard near the entrance, and visitors are told to wear a badge on campus, but there are no new fences or metal detectors.

Greg Dennis, who runs security for the district, says it's hard to reach consensus on what precautions to take.

"From a parent's perspective, they say, 'Holy cow, why aren't we doing this? Why aren't we building prisons, why aren't we building moats?'" Dennis says. "And the next person says, 'We can't do that! This is public property, you have to make it accessible, how do we use the playgrounds on the weekend?'"

Without the money to rebuild the school, administrators have opted to emphasize training and preparedness. They try to think tactically—for instance, since the shooting in Parkland, they've been reconsidering how to conduct fire drills, to make kids less of a target to potential attackers as they leave their classes.

But Marysville staffers also try to keep the risk in perspective. Dennis says he tries to learn security lessons from other shootings, but he doesn't want to obsess about them.

Madysen Pruss, who's part of a federally-funded counseling program at the school, says that's also her message to students when another shooting is in the news.

"We talk about how it's publicized through social media," Pruss says. "So it makes the threat feel greater than it is."

This year's seniors were freshmen when the shooting happened, so this is the last class that still has memories of the incident. Senior Olivya Cerdinio is one of a group of students who organized the school's observance of the 1-month milestone since the shooting in Parkland.

"I'm like kind of done being sad about it, and I'm just really mad about it, and I want to make a change," she says.

But it's shootings in general that she's mad about—not school shootings in particular.

"It's not dangerous because of how schools are," Cerdinio says, "but because a shooting can happen anywhere. It's more about gun availability."

EVALUATING THE AUTHOR'S ARGUMENTS:

In this viewpoint, Martin Kaste quotes a variety of sources on the subject of school shootings. Do you agree with his assertion that school shootings are not increasing? Support your reasoning with statistics from the viewpoint article.

Some Students Are Encouraged to Protest School Gun Violence

Tovia Smith

> *"Life is all about choices, and every choice has a consequence whether it be positive or negative."*

In the following viewpoint, Tovia Smith examines the various responses around the country from school officials over student protests of gun violence. Ahead of a national protest nicknamed "Walkout Wednesday" many school administrators weighed the best way to handle the disruption to their schedule. As the author notes, some students are punished because of protesting, while in other instances they are rewarded for such actions. Tovia Smith is an award-winning correspondent for National Public Radio.

AS YOU READ, CONSIDER THE FOLLOWING QUESTIONS:

1. According to the author what is the general response from colleges towards protesters?
2. As stated by the author, what is an example of punishment for protesting?
3. In the viewpoint one school official uses the word "anarchy" to describe protesting. What is meant by this?

After last month's mass shooting a Florida high school, students around the nation have staged walk-outs, rallies and other demonstrations to advocate for stricter gun measures. In response, some school administrators have threatened to suspend students who protest, and are being criticized for cracking down too hard. At the same time, many colleges are sending the opposite message, encouraging and congratulating students' activism.

In Boston, New Mission High School junior Ariyana Jones says many students at her school have been scared off from participating.

"Teachers will tell you straight up if you walk out, you will get written up and suspended," she says. "They are trying to intimidate us, and I feel like it's working because they don't want to get that on their record or get in trouble."

Needville, Texas Superintendent Curtis Rhodes, was more explicit, posting a warning on Facebook forbidding demonstrations during school hours, and threatening 3-day suspensions for anyone taking part. "Life is all about choices, and every choice has a consequence whether it be positive or negative," he wrote. "We will discipline no matter it if is one, fifty or five hundred students involved... and parent notes will not alleviate the discipline."

The post has since been taken down, and the school declined comment, but the warning got students worried—and got lawyers involved.

"Really what that is, is retaliation for a student expressing their first amendment rights," says Texas ACLU Staff Attorney Kali Cohen. She says the hard line approach is not only unconstitutional, but also flies in the face of public schools' mission, as affirmed by the U.S. Supreme Court, to prepare young people to be engaged citizens.

And colleges couldn't agree more. Scores of colleges have posted and tweeted to reassure students that if they get suspended for taking part in a peaceful protest, it will not diminish their chances of getting accepted. As MIT put it, students do not have to "choose between speaking out and getting in."

Brandeis echoed the sentiment, tweeting "#Brandeis supports students' right to stand up for their beliefs." The tweet not only assured students their admission would not be jeopardized if they

Protesting school gun violence during the 2018 National School Walkout Day allowed students to make their voices heard.

were disciplined for peaceful protest, but the tweet went further to urge them to go for it, saying "Speak up, speak out."

Brandeis says such activism, not only won't hurt students' chances of getting accepted, but may actually help.

"Having the bravery to stand up, to organize people, that takes a lot of courage and that is certainly something that I think would be applauded here," said Brandeis University Dean of Admissions Jennifer Walker. "From a Brandeis perspective, I think speaking up and speaking out is a good fit for our campus culture."

Students like Michael Martinez, a junior at Weston High School in Massachusetts, are taking comfort in the overwhelming support from colleges. Having personally lost a close relative and a family friend to gun violence, he's volunteering to help coordinate students across Massachusetts to join the National Walk-Out planned for March 14. "We want this to be more than just a march," Martinez says. He's organizing an afternoon of lobbying at the State House, to follow the walk out.

"This is an opportunity for students to really, really get involved in a way that I don't think a lot of students have ever been before," he says. "Young people to practice civic responsibility, service, community leadership and advocacy. I mean, it's a real life lesson, and a lot more valuable than anything a student would be learning in a classroom that day."

Student organizer Vikiana Petit-Homme, a junior at Boston Latin Academy, agrees.

"Schools should be encouraging youth to speak," she says. "They are there to prepare kids for the future, and [that means] learning to make sure we're heard. They should not be silencing us."

The outcry from students and parents and the response from colleges seems to have prompted some high schools to soften their stance.

In Virginia, the Prince William County schools sent out a letter last month warning students that those who disrupt classes or leave school without permission will face disciplinary action. But after a bit of a uproar, officials sent a second letter the next day saying they had "clearly sent the wrong message" and promising to "allow for some flexibility."

But neither can it just be anarchy, says Associate Superintendent Phil Kavits; Schools have to balance students' rights with student safety.

"There have been examples in the past where people have had walk outs and decided to march down busy streets," Kavits says. "And when they do that, we've lost the ability to keep them safe."

Just this week, some 700 middle school students staged a walk out, after informing school officials that it was coming, and getting their blessing.

In Boston, high school students gathered to plan their March 14 walk out were waiting to hear how friendly their administrators would be to the idea, when School Superintendent Tommy Chang popped in unexpectedly, and pleasantly surprised them. He praised their work, and assured them they will not be disciplined for it.

It was welcome news to students like Petit-Homme. But she's quick to add, no official policy would have stopped her anyway.

"At this point, we've seen the adults are not doing what they're supposed to be doing, which is to keep us safe," she says. "So we're done with going to them and asking for permission. At this point we're just going to do what we have to."

Yes, Petit-Homme says, protests will be peaceful, but she says students cannot promise that they'll never disrupt the school day.

"The whole point is to be disruptive, to make sure we catch your attention. It's to make sure that you are hearing us. So causing a disruption is exactly what we're going for."

There's no guarantee if, or when, it may result in real change. But it will almost certainly make for a college application essay the admissions committee will love.

EVALUATING THE AUTHOR'S ARGUMENTS:

In this viewpoint, Tovia Smith reports on the consequences of student protesting of gun violence. From the viewpoint article it appears there is a distinct difference between the feelings of colleges and high schools on what is appropriate. What are the differences? Provide examples from the viewpoint article to answer this question.

Statistics About School Shootings Don't Always Represent the Truth

"There is no way to know how many school shootings... have occurred outside of the United States over the past 20 years."

Tom Kertscher

In the following viewpoint, Tom Kertscher argues that we must be careful when interpreting data surrounding school shootings. The author analyzes claims made on Twitter about statistical issues surrounding school shootings. He focuses on a statistical claim and points out the inaccuracies of the claim. Kertscher provides ample evidence, demonstrating how some statistics can lead to false assumptions. Tom Kertscher writes for the *Journal Sentinel*. For Politifact Wisconsin, he covers issues related to government and courts.

AS YOU READ, CONSIDER THE FOLLOWING QUESTIONS:
1. According to the author what is the basic statistical issue being analyzed?
2. How are misleading statistics being echoed by other news media as stated in the viewpoint?
3. What does "research" have to do with statistics in this viewpoint?

"Mostly False: 18 U.S. School Shootings So Far in 2018 and 18 in Rest of the World Over Past 20 Years," by Tom Kertscher, The Poynter Institute, February 15, 2018. Reprinted by permission.

A mid the early news reports about a Florida school shooting that left 17 dead on Feb. 14, 2018, longtime network TV journalist and author Jeff Greenfield declared in a tweet:

In the rest of the world, there have been 18 school shootings in the last twenty years. In the U.S., there have been 18 school shootings since January 1.

It's a provocative claim that drew more the 130,000 likes on Twitter.

Greenfield, a University of Wisconsin-Madison graduate, may be on the right track generally in contrasting how much gun violence there is in America compared to the rest of the world.

But as for his specific claim, he leaves a misleading impression with the U.S. part and lacks evidence for the part about the rest of the world.

U.S. School Shootings

On the U.S. part of his claim, Greenfield told us his 18 school shootings in 2018 comes from the Everytown for Gun Safety Support Fund, as reported by ABC News.

We found that in the immediate aftermath of the shooting at Marjory Stoneman Douglas High School, Politico, TIME, CNBC and other national media also reported on Everytown's 18 figure. In addition, the New York Daily News claimed 18 school shootings, listing the same incidents as Everytown, and HuffPost reported 18, too.

But there are some major caveats to that figure.

Indeed, when we asked Greenfield for information to back up his claim, he noted to us in his email that the Everytown group's count "conflates very different incidents, from the harmless to the deadly."

As PolitiFact National has reported, Everytown, an advocacy group co-founded by former New York Mayor Michael Bloomberg that seeks to prevent gun violence, uses a broad definition of school shooting—that is, any time a firearm discharges a live round inside a school building, or on a school campus or grounds. Its database includes incidents when no one was injured; attempted or completed suicide, with no intent to injure others; and cases when a gun

Mass shootings occur much more frequently in the United States than in other nations.

was fired unintentionally, resulting in injury or death. The list also includes incidents on college campuses.

As we'll see, Everytown counts shooting incidents that are dramatically different than what happened in Florida:

So, there are 18 incidents in which a gun was fired inside a school or on school property.

Three—Italy, Texas, Kentucky and Florida—were mass shootings. But of the other shootings:

- Nine involved no deaths and no gunshot injuries.
- Two were suicides, with no other injuries (including the one at the closed school).
- Three were unintentional (although one caused injuries).

Rest of the World

As PolitiFact National has noted, mass shootings do happen in other countries. But they do not happen with the same frequency as in the United States.

Two researchers—Jaclyn Schildkraut of the State University of New York in Oswego and H. Jaymi Elsass of Texas State University

2018 US school shootings as counted by Everytown

Date	Place	Details
Jan. 3	East Olive Elementary, St. Johns, Mich.	Man committed suicide in parking lot. No other injuries. (We found the building was not being used as a school, as East Olive had been shut down more than six months earlier.)
Jan. 4	New Start High, Seattle	Unidentified shooter fired shots into building. No injuries.
Jan. 10	Grayson College, Denison, Texas	Student unintentionally fired a bullet from gun legally possessed by an instructor that struck a wall. No injuries.
Jan. 10	Coronado Elementary, Sierra Vista, Ariz.	Student committed suicide in bathroom. No other injuries.
Jan. 10	California State University, San Bernardino	Gunshots, most likely fired from off campus, hit a campus building window. No injuries.
Jan. 15	Wiley College, Marshall, Texas	Shots fired from car in parking lot, with one shot hitting window of residence hall. No injuries.
Jan. 20	Wake Forest University, Winston-Salem, N.C.	One student wounds another student during argument at sorority party.
Jan. 22	Italy High, Italy, Texas	Student opens fire in cafeteria, wounding one student before firing at another student and missing.
Jan. 22	NET Charter High, Gentilly, La.	Unknown person fired shots at students standing in parking lot. No injuries from gunshots.
Jan. 23	Marshall County High, Benton, Ky.	2 students left dead in mass shooting by student. More than a dozen students injured.
Jan. 25	Murphy High, Mobile, Ala.	Student fired into the air outside school after argument in school. No injuries.
Jan. 26	Dearborn High, Dearborn, Mich.	Individual ejected from game for fighting was shot at in parking lot. No injuries.
Jan. 31	Lincoln High, Philadelphia	Man fatally wounded in fight in parking lot.
Feb. 1	Salvador B. Castro Middle, Los Angeles	Student unintentionally fires gun in classroom, wounds two students.
Feb. 5	Oxon Hill High, Oxon Hill, Md.	Student wounded in parking lot during apparent robbery.
Feb. 5	Harmony Learning K-12, Maplewood, Minn.	Student pressed trigger on school liaison officer's gun. No injuries.
Feb. 8	Metropolitan High, New York, N.Y.	Student fired gun into floor in classroom. No injuries.
Feb. 14	Stoneman Douglas High, Parkland, Fla.	Ex-student allegedly commits mass shooting; 17 deaths.

—analyzed mass shootings in 11 countries, covering the period from 2000-14. Aside from the United States, they looked at Australia, Canada, China, England, Finland, France, Germany, Mexico, Norway and Switzerland.

The United States had more mass shootings—and more people cumulatively killed or injured—than the other 10 nations combined, according to their research. While part of this is because the United States has a much bigger population than all but China, the difference can't be explained by skewed population numbers alone.

But as for the other part of Greenfield's claim—that there have been only 18 school shootings in the rest of the world over the past 20 years—Greenfield told us he couldn't recall the source of that information, adding, "yes, I cop to insufficient research."

Mark Bryant, executive director of the Gun Violence Archive (which the New York Times uses to track school shooting data), told us the 18-shootings figure could be correct in terms of how many mass shootings occur in schools outside of the United States that get widespread news coverage.

But Bryant said there is no way to know—based on the definition of school shootings that Greenfield relies on—how many such shootings occur around the globe.

About 24 hours after posting the tweet, Greenfield took it down.

Our Rating

In the wake of a Florida school shooting that left 17 people dead, Greenfield said: "In the rest of the world, there have been 18 school shootings in the last twenty years. In the U.S., there have been 18 school shootings since January 1."

By one count widely cited in the news media, there have been 18 incidents in which shots were fired inside or outside of a school or university building in the United States so far in 2018. But only three involved a mass shooting. And the count includes two suicides, three accidental shootings and nine incidents in which there were no fatalities or injuries.

As for the rest of the world, Greenfield had no evidence to back up that part of his claim. And an expert relied on by the New York Times for gun violence statistics told us there is no way to know how many school shootings—using the definition Greenfield relies on—have occurred outside of the United States over the past 20 years.

For a statement that contains only an element of truth, our rating is Mostly False.

EVALUATING THE AUTHOR'S ARGUMENTS:

In this viewpoint Tom Kertscher analyzes a statistic tweeted out by a longtime journalist. Kertscher judges it to be false. Do you agree or disagree with the author? Back up your claims with details from the viewpoint.

School Shootings Are a Concern for American Teens and Parents

"A majority of American teens say they are very or somewhat worried about the possibility of a shooting happening at their school."

Nikki Graf

In the following viewpoint, Nikki Graf argues that most teens in America along with their parents are worried about school shootings happening in their own schools. Graf reports that teens have firm opinions on what will work to prevent further gun violence as do their parents. Graf points out gender and racial differences in how teens view the possibility of gun violence and how party affiliations, either Democratic or Republican, seem to play in thinking. Nikki Graf is a research associate at the Pew Research Center.

AS YOU READ, CONSIDER THE FOLLOWING QUESTIONS:

1. According to the author, what do teens want done to prevent gun violence?
2. Explain how the gender difference affects fear of gun violence.
3. As stated in the viewpoint, which groups favor arming teachers?

"A Majority of U.S. Teens Fear a Shooting Could Happen at Their School, and Most Parents Share Their Concern," by Nikki Graf, Pew Research Center, April 18, 2018.

In the aftermath of the deadly shooting at a high school in Parkland, Florida, a majority of American teens say they are very or somewhat worried about the possibility of a shooting happening at their school—and most parents of teens share that concern, according to new Pew Research Center surveys of teens ages 13 to 17 and parents with children in the same age range.

Meanwhile, when it comes to what can be done to prevent this kind of violence, far more teens view proposals focused on mental illness, assault-style weapon bans and the use of metal detectors in schools as potentially effective than say the same about allowing teachers and school officials to carry guns in schools.

The surveys of teens and parents were conducted in March and April 2018, following the Feb. 14 shooting at Marjory Stoneman Douglas High School—one of the deadliest mass school shootings in U.S. history. Seventeen people were killed in the attack and more than a dozen others were injured. The surveys also come as the nation prepares to mark the 19th anniversary of the shooting at Columbine High School in Colorado.

Overall, 57% of teens say they are worried about the possibility of a shooting happening at their school, with one-in-four saying they are very worried. About three-in-ten (29%) say they are not too worried about this, and just 13% say they are not at all worried.

Nonwhite teens express a higher level of concern than their white peers. Roughly two-thirds (64%) of nonwhite teens, including 73% of Hispanics, say they are at least somewhat worried about this, compared with 51% of white teens.

School shooting fears differ by gender as well: 64% of girls say they are very or somewhat worried about a shooting happening at their school, compared with 51% of boys.

Parents of teenagers express similar levels of concern as teens themselves, with 63% saying they are at least somewhat worried about the possibility of a shooting happening at their child's school. And there are similar patterns when it comes to race and gender, with nonwhite parents and mothers expressing more concern. Lower-income parents are particularly worried—in fact, 82% of parents with annual household incomes under $30,000 say they are at least somewhat worried that a shooting could happen at their teen's school, compared with

A sizeable percentage of teens today express concern that they will experience a shooting at school.

64% of those with incomes between $30,000 and $74,999 and 53% of those with incomes of $75,000 or more.

Some Policies Seen as More Effective than Others

Against the backdrop of organized school walkouts and marches calling for new legislation to address gun violence, teens see more value in some proposed measures than others. Asked to assess how effective various measures would be at preventing school shootings, 86% of teens say that preventing people with mental illnesses from purchasing guns and that improving mental health screening and treatment would be effective, including majorities who say each of these proposals would be very effective. Roughly eight-in-ten teens (79%) say that having metal detectors in schools would be effective and 66% say the same about banning assault-style weapons.

By contrast, a much smaller share of teens (39%) say that allowing teachers to carry guns in schools would be very or somewhat effective at preventing school shootings; 35% of teens say this would be not at all effective.

Black teens are far less likely than white and Hispanic teens to say allowing teachers to carry guns in schools would be at least somewhat effective: 23% of black teens say this, compared with 44% of white teens and 39% of Hispanic teens.

Views on the effectiveness of banning assault-style weapons also differ by race and ethnicity. About eight-in-ten black teens (80%) and Hispanic teens (79%) say this would be at least somewhat effective; a smaller share of white teens say the same (59%). And while teens across racial and ethnic groups are about equally likely to see metal detectors as effective, black teens are far more likely than their white and Hispanic counterparts to say this would be very effective (59% vs. 39% and 41%, respectively).

Partisan Divide Among Adults

Teens' views on proposals to prevent school shootings mirror those of the general public, for the most part.

Among all adults, opinions on arming teachers and banning assault-style weapons diverge sharply along party lines, according to a separate Pew Research Center survey also conducted in March and April. (The survey of teens did not ask respondents for their partisan affiliations.)

About eight-in-ten Republicans and Republican-leaning independents (78%) say that allowing teachers to carry guns in schools would be very or somewhat effective at preventing school shootings, compared with just 24% of Democrats and Democratic-leaning independents. Democrats, on the other hand, are far more likely than Republicans to say that banning assault-style weapons would be at least somewhat effective (81% vs. 35%).

But there are some points of partisan agreement—substantial majorities of both Democrats and Republicans say that proposals directed at mental illness and having metal detectors in schools have the potential to be at least somewhat effective in preventing school shootings.

EVALUATING THE AUTHOR'S ARGUMENTS:

In this viewpoint Nikki Graf analyzes how teens and parents feel about the possibility of a shooting occurring at their school. How do you feel personally about this? Compare and contrast your beliefs about what could make the situation safer with the viewpoint statistics.

Ask the Secret Service How to Prevent School Shootings

"Schools that prevented a shooting had done some of the things recommended by the Secret Service."

Jeff Daniels

In the following viewpoint, Jeff Daniels argues that credible research on how to prevent school shootings was done by the US Secret Service shortly after the school shooting in Columbine. Daniels analyzes the report and concludes that there are many possible warning behaviors that a potential school shooter may display and that authorities must have enough power to intervene when someone appears to be on a troubling path to violence. Besides writing and researching on violence prevention, Jeff Daniels is a professor of counseling psychology at West Virginia University.

AS YOU READ, CONSIDER THE FOLLOWING QUESTIONS:

1. What is the "process" of a school shooting, according to the viewpoint?
2. As reported by the author, school shooters are most commonly from what gender and racial identity?
3. Identify three possible warning behaviors that shooters display as stated by the author.

W While President Donald Trump has not shied away from offering suggestions on how to prevent school shootings —including one controversial idea to arm teachers— what often gets overlooked in the conversation is research on the subject that has already been done.

This research includes one major study of school shootings conducted in part by the very agency charged with protecting the president of the United States himself - the U.S. Secret Service.

Has this research been ignored or just forgotten? I raise the question as one who has studied averted school shootings and the news coverage that followed.

Two months after the Columbine tragedy in 1999, experts from the U.S. Department of Education and the U.S. Secret Service collaborated to study the "school shooter" phenomenon. They published the study on their findings in 2002. The study focused on examining the thinking, planning and other behaviors of students who carried out school attacks. Particular attention was given to identifying pre-attack behaviors and communications that might be detectable —or "knowable —and could help prevent future attacks.

The team studied 37 school shootings involving 41 attackers that took place from December 1974 through May 2000. Data included investigative, school, court and mental health records. In addition, 10 school shooters were interviewed to gain their perspectives from "conceptualization to execution" of the attacks. A series of findings emerged. In light of the Florida school shooting massacre and the fact that the alleged shooter drew a lot of attention prior to carrying out the shooting, those findings bear repeating here.

"Incidents of targeted violence at school rarely were sudden, impulsive acts."

Most attackers progressed through a process that started with an idea, to a plan, to accessing weapons and ending with the attack. If noticed, this process may be interrupted at any time before the attack.

A study by the Secret Service provided recommendations that can help avert school shootings.

"Prior to most incidents, other people knew about the attacker's idea and/or plan to attack."

The implication is that schools must develop a culture that promotes student sharing of concerns about others. In studying schools that averted a shooting, I and other researchers found that a key factor was establishing trusting relationships with students. We also found that the notion of "snitching" needed to be reframed to being helpful. Unfortunately, it seems that in the case of the Parkland shooting, multiple people did come forward with concerns. The alleged shooter was on several different radars, but unless he was posing an imminent danger to himself or others, he couldn't be jailed or forced to receive psychological services. It therefore becomes an issue of individual versus collective rights. Unless we are ready as a society to lock people up for disturbing communications, there will be some individuals who will fall through the proverbial cracks.

Along similar lines, most attackers "engaged in some behavior prior to the incident that caused others concern or indicated a need for help."

Some of these behaviors included talking about bringing a gun to school, or warning friends to avoid a certain area of the school on a given day. The Parkland shooter had a history of violent and aggressive behavior, including Instagram posts about becoming a "professional school shooter."

While most attackers—96 percent—were male, the report found that there "is no accurate or useful 'profile' of students who engaged in targeted school violence."

Three-quarters of the attackers were white; one-quarter of the attackers came from other racial and ethnic backgrounds, including African-American (12 percent), Hispanic (5 percent), Native Alaskan (2 percent), Native American (2 percent) and Asian (2 percent). Most came from intact families, were doing well in school and were not loners, according to the report.

"Most attackers had difficulty coping with significant losses or personal failures. Moreover, many had considered or attempted suicide."

Knowing the students and what they are dealing with in their lives, such as parental divorce, ending of a relationship or other failures is important for getting help in a timely manner. The Parkland shooter's adoptive mother died of pneumonia just three months prior to his deadly attack. And at age 5, he also witnessed his father die of a heart attack.

"Many attackers felt bullied, persecuted or injured by others prior to the attack."

Almost two-thirds reported being targeted by others prior to the attack, with some claiming to have withstood severe bullying for a long time. There is evidence that Nikolas Cruz was often mocked for his odd behavior.

Following the publication of the Secret Service study on school shootings, my research on averted school shootings found that schools that prevented a shooting had done some of the things recommended by the Secret Service.

The case in Florida shows that many of these recommendations were followed and people spoke up when they saw something wrong. The issue is whether authorities need more power to intervene once they have been made aware of a potential threat, or whether they just need to do a better job with the power they already have.

EVALUATING THE AUTHOR'S ARGUMENTS:

In this viewpoint Jeff Daniels reiterates information provided by the US Secret Service on what to watch for in determining if an individual might be a possible school shooter. Do you think school administrators have enough power to restrain someone they suspect of having violent tendencies? Why or why not?

Viewpoint

6

School Shootings Have Long-Term Effects

"Extensive research suggests that exposure to violence can affect children's health and well-being for years into the future."

Denise-Marie Ordway

In the following viewpoint, Denise-Marie Ordway argues that school shooting violence adversely affects the lives of children long after the event occurs. Ordway analyzes the issue by including specific case studies from the United States and around the world. The studies she cites provide details about specific violent incidents and the measured effects suffered by children that are involved in violence or witness to such acts. Denise-Marie Ordway writes for the Shorenstein Center on Media, Politics and Public Policy.

AS YOU READ, CONSIDER THE FOLLOWING QUESTIONS:

1. How do children who experience physical violence react? Cite two examples from the viewpoint.
2. What can happen to children living in violent communities as reported by the author?
3. What typically happens to private schools after a school shooting event?

B efore the end of February 2018, dozens of students were killed or injured in school shootings in Kentucky and Florida. The previous year, fatal shootings rocked campuses in Ohio, New Mexico, California and other states.

As reporters rush to collect facts, they also try to put these events into context, focusing, for example, on questions about gun policies and how local communities are grappling with the sudden deaths of children, teachers and coaches.

Long after news crews leave, though, those who witnessed these tragedies will bear their consequences. Extensive research suggests that exposure to violence can affect children's health and well-being for years into the future. It also can desensitize them, leading them to see violence as an acceptable way to deal with problems.

Below, we have pulled together research that looks at other impacts that might seem less obvious to reporters covering the issue. These studies offer insights into how student performance and school enrollments may change following a shooting.

We also have included resources aimed at helping journalists improve their coverage of school shootings, including tips on interviewing children and an explainer on firearm technology and vocabulary.

"The Relationships Between Violence in Childhood and Educational Outcomes: A Global Systematic Review and Meta-analysis"

From the University of Edinburgh, China Agricultural University, Georgia State University and the Centre for Population Health Sciences, published in Child Abuse & Neglect, 2018. By Deborah Fry, Xiangming Fang, Stuart Elliott, Tabitha Casey, Xiaodong Zheng, Jiaoyuan Li, Lani Florian and Gillean McCluskey.

This research article examines dozens of studies from 21 countries to understand the relationship between different types of violence in childhood and a range of education-related outcomes such as academic performance, absenteeism and graduation and dropout rates. The study finds that all types of childhood violence have an impact. For example, children who experience physical violence are

Children and teens should be able to focus on learning while at school. Studies show that students experiencing violence are compromised academically.

20 percent less likely to graduate. Children who experience any type of violence are less likely to earn high grades and test scores.

"The Effect of Community Traumatic Events on Student Achievement: Evidence from the Beltway Sniper Attacks"

From American University, published in Education Finance and Policy, May 2017. By Seth Gershenson and Erdal Tekin.

This study looks at how traumatic events such as mass shootings affect the performance of students living in the community where the events occurred. Gershenson and Tekin focused specifically on how elementary school students in Virginia performed on standardized tests after the "Beltway Sniper" attacks of 2002. "The main results indicate that the attacks significantly reduced school-level proficiency rates in schools within five miles of an attack. Evidence of a causal effect is most robust for math proficiency rates in the third and fifth grades, and third grade reading proficiency, suggesting that the shootings caused a decline in school proficiency rates of about 2 to 5 percent. Particularly concerning from an equity standpoint, these effects appear to be entirely driven by achievement declines in schools that serve higher proportions of racial minority and socioeconomically disadvantaged students."

"The Effect of High School Shootings on Schools and Student Performance"

From Louisiana State University and University of Missouri, published in Educational Evaluation and Policy Analysis, March 2016. By Louis-Philippe Beland and Dongwoo Kim.

This study suggests that high schools where fatal shootings have occurred experience a 5.8 percent drop in freshmen enrollment, on average, following the event. The researchers also examined standardized test scores in California and found that scores in math and English declined for students who remain enrolled after the shooting. Beland and Kim did not find statistically significant impacts on graduation or suspension rates or student attendance.

"School Shootings and Private School Enrollment"

From the University of Wisconsin-Milwaukee, published in Economics Letters, February 2013. By Rahi Abouk and Scott Adams.

This study finds that school shootings increase enrollment at private high schools, particularly in suburban and rural areas. The researchers looked at enrollment at public and private high schools nationwide between 1998 and 2009 and matched that data with school shooting reports. Private school enrollments increased an estimated 9.7-11.6 percent in the academic year immediately following a shooting. Meanwhile, public school enrollment fell an estimated 0.4-1.3 percent. "Parents overestimate the potential for such events to be repeated, particularly those that occur in suburban and rural areas, because of intense media coverage," the authors write.

EVALUATING THE AUTHOR'S ARGUMENTS:

In this viewpoint Denise-Marie Ordway contends that children exposed to gun violence suffer long after the incident. Some parents react to this violence by removing their children from public school. What advice would you give to these parents instead?

Chapter 2

What Causes School Shootings?

School shootings have been blamed on easy access to guns, mental health issues, lack of security, exposure to violence, and problems that arise from social media, among other reasons.

Mass Killing Is Caused by More Than Just Guns

"Are there ways to reduce gun violence and school shootings? Yes, but only after objectively assessing the facts and working collaboratively to fashion common-sense solutions."

John G. Malcolm and Amy Swearer

In the following viewpoint, John G. Malcolm and Amy Swearer argue that guns should not be the focus of debates about mass killings. Clearly defining terms surrounding gun violence and mass killing, the authors debate the common topics of mental illness, gun control, and occurrence of gun violence outside the United States. They provide evidence demonstrating that mass killings outside the United States often kill more than the mass shootings in the United States. John G. Malcom is vice president of the Institute for Constitutional Government. Amy Swearer is a legal policy analyst at the Heritage Foundation.

AS YOU READ, CONSIDER THE FOLLOWING QUESTIONS:
1. What is the difference between "mass shooting" and "mass public shooting" according to the authors?
2. Will gun control work to lessen shootings?
3. What is a commonality shared by people who have committed mass killings?

"6 Reasons Gun Control Will Not Solve Mass Killings," by John G. Malcolm and Amy Swearer, Daily Signal, March 16, 2018. Reprinted by permission.

In the wake of the tragic murder of 17 innocent students and teachers at Marjory Stoneman Douglas High School in Parkland, Florida, students, educators, politicians, and activists are searching for solutions to prevent future school shootings.

As emotions morph from grief to anger to resolve, it is vitally important to supply facts so that policymakers and professionals can fashion solutions based on objective data rather than well-intended but misguided emotional fixes.

Are there ways to reduce gun violence and school shootings? Yes, but only after objectively assessing the facts and working collaboratively to fashion common-sense solutions.

Definitions

"Mass shooting" typically refers to mass killings where the assailant used a firearm or firearms. In 2013, Congress defined "mass killing" as "3 or more killings in a single incident."

A prominent 2017 study defined "mass public shootings" as incidents that occur in the absence of other criminal activity (such as robberies, drug deals, and gang-related turf wars) in which a gun is used to kill four or more victims at a public location.

Mass killings are rare, and mass public shootings are even rarer.

Mass killings are very rare, accounting for only 0.2 percent of homicides every year and approximately 1 percent of homicide victims.

Only 12 percent of mass killings are mass public shootings. Most mass killings are familicides (murders of family members or intimate partners) and felony-related killings (such as robberies gone awry or gang-related "turf battles").

Although there has been a slight increase in the frequency of mass public shootings over the past few years, the rates are still similar to what the United States experienced in the 1980s and early 1990s.

Many gun control measures are not likely to be helpful.

Over 90 percent of public mass shootings take place in "gun-free zones" where civilians are not permitted to carry firearms.

Assault rifles are readily available at most gun shows, where sellers are not required to perform background checks on buyers in what's known as the "gunshow loophole."

A complete ban on "assault weapons" will save very few lives: Six out of every 10 mass public shootings are carried out by handguns alone, while only one in 10 is committed with a rifle alone.

The average age of mass public shooters is 34, which means that increasing the minimum age for purchasing firearms would not target the main perpetrators of mass public shootings.

Few mass public shooters have used "high-capacity magazines," and there is no evidence that the lethality of their attacks would have been affected by delays of two to four seconds to switch magazines. In fact, some of the largest mass shootings in U.S. history were carried out with "low-capacity" weapons:

- The Virginia Tech shooter killed 32 and injured 17 with two handguns, one of which had a 10-round magazine and the other a 15-round magazine. He simply brought 19 extra magazines.

- Twenty-three people were killed and another 20 injured in a Killeen, Texas, cafeteria by a man with two 9mm handguns, capable of maximums of 15-round and 17-round magazines, respectively.
- A mentally disturbed man armed with two handguns and a shotgun shot and killed 21 people in a San Ysidro McDonald's and injured another 19.

The handguns utilized 13-round and 20-round magazines, and the shotgun had a five-round capacity.

Public mass shooters typically have histories of mental health issues.

According to one study, 60 percent of mass public shooters had been diagnosed with a mental disorder or had demonstrated signs of serious mental illness prior to the attack.

A large body of research shows a statistical link between mass public killings and serious untreated psychiatric illness. The most commonly diagnosed illnesses among mass public shooters are paranoid schizophrenia and severe depression.

It is important to remember that the vast majority of people with mental disorders do not engage in violent behaviors, and there is no empirical means of effectively identifying potential mass murderers.

The United States does not have an extraordinary problem with mass public shootings compared to other developed countries.

After adjusting for population differences, many other developed countries have worse problems with mass public shootings than the United States has.

There were 27 percent more casualties per capita from mass public shootings in the European Union than in the U.S. from 2009 to 2015.

Mass killers often find ways to kill even without firearms.

Some of the worst mass killings in the United States have occurred without firearms:

- Before the 2016 Orlando nightclub shooting, the deadliest attack on the LGBT community in America occurred in 1973 when an arsonist killed 32 and injured 15 at the Upstairs Lounge in New Orleans.
- In 1987, a disgruntled former airline employee killed 43 people after he hijacked and intentionally crashed a passenger plane.
- In 1990, an angry ex-lover burned down the Happy Land social club where his former girlfriend worked, killing 87 others in the process.
- In 1995, 168 people were killed and more than 600 were injured by a truck bomb parked outside the Alfred P. Murrah Federal Building in Oklahoma City, Oklahoma.
- In 2017, a man in New York City killed eight and injured 11 by renting a truck and plowing down pedestrians on a Manhattan bike path.

In other countries, bombings, mass stabbings, and car attacks frequently kill more people than even the deadliest mass shootings in the United States. Consider the following:

- Spain (2004) — Bombing: 192 deaths, 2,050 injuries;
- Great Britain (2005) — Bombing: 52 deaths, 784 injuries;
- Japan (2008) — Car ramming and stabbing: seven deaths, 10 injuries;
- China (2010) — Shovel-loader: 11 deaths, 30 injuries;
- China (2014) — Car ramming: six deaths, 13 injuries;
- China (2014) — Mass stabbing: 31 deaths, 143 injuries;
- Germany (2015) — Plane crash: 150 deaths;
- Belgium (2016) — Bombing: 21 deaths, 180 injuries;
- France (2016) — Car ramming: 86 deaths, 434 injuries;
- Germany (2016) — Car ramming: 11 deaths, 56 injuries;
- Japan (2016) — Mass stabbing: 19 deaths, 45 injuries; and
- Great Britain (2017) — Bombing: 22 deaths, 250 injuries.

Australia did not "eliminate mass public shootings" by banning assault weapons.

Australia did not "eliminate mass public shootings" by banning assault weapons. Mass shootings in the country were rare before the 1996 National Firearms Act, and multiple-casualty shootings still occur.

Before 1996, firearms crimes in Australia rarely involved firearms prohibited under the National Firearms Act, suggesting that any change in firearm-related crimes or deaths was not due to the law.

Further, Australia did not see a reduction in "mass murders." In the years immediately following enactment of the National Firearms Act, the country experienced six mass murders in which five or more people were killed—they just were not killed with guns.

EVALUATING THE AUTHORS' ARGUMENTS:

Viewpoint authors Malcolm and Swearer give many reasons why they believe that gun control might not decrease mass killings. Using specific details from the viewpoint construct an argument that supports the authors' conclusions.

Proposed Gun Laws Would Not Have Stopped Recent Shootings

"Of the 12 mass shootings during 2012 and 2015, nine would not have been stopped by any proposed gun control laws."

Lucille Eleanor Nguyen

In the following viewpoint, Lucille Eleanor Nguyen contends that proposed gun legislation would not have stopped many of the recent incidents of gun violence. Nguyen argues that universal background checks, weapons bans, or ammunition purchase limits would not do any good in stemming the killing. Instead, the author insists that other causes are behind this societal problem. Lucille Eleanor Nguyen is a contributing writer for the *Oberlin Review.*

AS YOU READ, CONSIDER THE FOLLOWING QUESTIONS:

1. According to the author, why would universal background checks not have stopped this shooting?
2. How do shooters get around ammunition restrictions as reported in the viewpoint?
3. What are two causes of the proliferation of gun violence in the opinion of the author?

Like every other American, I was shocked and horrified to hear the news that 17 people had been killed in yet another mass shooting. The stories of the brave people at Marjory Stoneman High School who gave their lives to save others—like Peter Wang, only 15 years old, who was killed holding open the door so that his fellow students could escape to safety—are a testament to the indomitable human spirit that persists in even the worst of circumstances. They deserve our memory, our respect, and our action.

Something should be done. Something needs to be done. Something has to be done.

Unfortunately, I'm not sure that the legislative proposals that are being put forward today by our representatives would even be effective at stopping attacks like this. I hoped that my intuition was incorrect, but the harsh truth is that no popular gun control policy proposed today—or that has been previously proposed—would have stopped this shooting.

Universal background checks would not have stopped this shooting. The man accused of this heinous act went to a Federal Firearms Licensed gun store, filled out what is known as a Form 4473 Firearms Transaction Record, and was approved by the National Criminal Background Check System created by the FBI. According to the special agent in charge for the Miami division of the Bureau of Alcohol, Tobacco, Firearms, and Explosives, Peter J Forcelli, "no laws were violated in the procurement of this weapon."

An assault weapons ban would not have stopped this shooting. Nick Cruz committed last week's killings with an AR-15 style semi-automatic "assault" rifle—one of the most popular civilian rifles available to the general public, with an estimated 5 million AR-15s in civilian hands. Most firearms experts agree that previous legislation on assault weapons focused on mostly cosmetic features of a rifle—pistol grips, telescoping stocks, handguards, flash hiders, bayonet mounts, vertical foregrips, etc.—and did nothing to address the lethality of the weapons themselves. A commonly available semi-automatic rifle known as the Ruger Mini-14 was available during the 1994 Federal Assault Weapons Ban until the ban's mandatory expiration in 2003; it was just as lethal as the AR-15 and had a similar rate of fire. The only difference? It's a gun made of wood and metal, free of any of

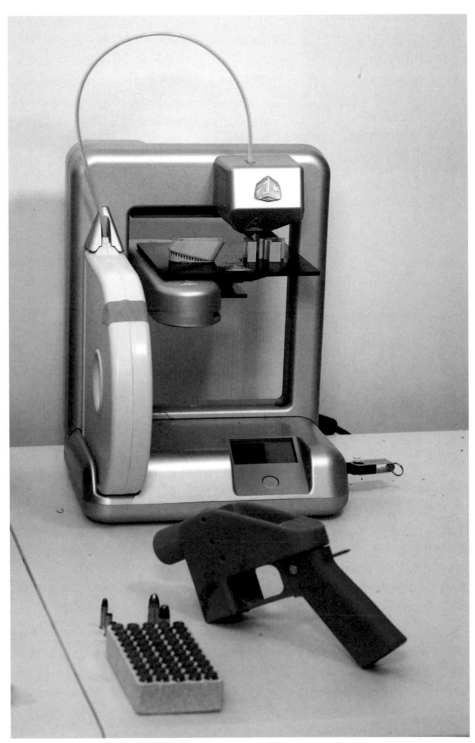

Gun control advocates are outraged at the prospect of 3D-printed firearms.

the features that any state or federal law would classify as an assault weapon.

A magazine restriction capacity would not have stopped this shooting. Even if this shooter was restricted to 10 round magazines, an experienced shooter could easily replace a magazine in two to four seconds. A review by Gary Kleck of Florida State University found that of 23 mass shootings—defined as more than six deaths—between 1994 and 2003, when a magazine restriction of ten rounds was mandated by the Federal Assault Weapons Ban, only one stopped while reloading and all 23 had multiple weapons. The shooter at Marjory Stoneman had multiple minutes of uninterrupted shooting between when he started and when he was arrested by the police. It is unlikely that multiple magazines would have impeded his rampage.

Killers could easily subvert ammunition purchase limits by amassing a large amount of ammunition over a longer span of time. Requiring weapon microstamping, which involves firing pin imprinting specific indentations on bullet casing, wouldn't have stopped a mass shooting. Gun safes wouldn't have stopped this mass shooting—although they may have prevented shooters from obtaining their weapons by acquiring them from other gun owners. Enhanced mental health treatments wouldn't have stopped this shooting—the shooter had, reportedly, previously been in therapy. Gun licenses wouldn't have stopped this shooting—this shooter passed all legal requirements to own a gun. Waiting periods between the purchase of a firearm and time of possession likely would not have stopped this shooter—he had reportedly planned this attack for quite some time.

I'm not alone in this analysis. Glenn Kessler of The Washington Post's "Fact Checker" blog analyzed mass shootings between 2012 and 2015, finding that of the 12 mass shootings during that period, nine would not have been stopped by any proposed gun control laws. The other three had more nuanced findings: The Dec. 14, 2012 Newtown Elementary School shooting might have been prevented if the shooter wasn't able to access his mother's firearms, and the AR-15 rifle—one of many weapons used in the shooting—might have been made illegal under a failed 2013 assault weapons ban; the June 7, 2013 Santa Monica shooting involved a person who built their own firearms and circumvented federal law; and the Dec. 2, 2015 San Bernardino shooting involved weapons modified to circumvent California law but were legal in most states under federal law.

So what should be done? Nobody has a good answer to that question. 33,000 people die every year from firearms, almost two-thirds of which are suicides. Only the remaining third is split between firearm murders and accidents. In fact, mass shootings only constituted one percent of firearm deaths between 1980 and 2008.

I am in favor of universal background checks for every firearm purchase, reasonable waiting periods, gun safe and lock requirements, and expanded access to mental health treatment. However, I recognize that mass shootings are an unfortunate consequence of the wide availability of firearms, the American culture of individualism, a desire for fame and notoriety, and the copycat phenomenon. The legislative solutions for those problems are much more difficult than anything that has been put forward so far.

We owe it to the victims to make the right choices when we request legislation from our representatives. It's easy to believe that if we just do a few things that we can totally eliminate mass shootings, but the reality is much more difficult. We must balance our idealism with our realism and face these difficult choices together, as one people. As Abraham Lincoln professed this month 158 years ago in his Cooper Union address, "let us have faith that right makes might, and in that faith, let us, to the end, dare to do our duty as we understand it."

EVALUATING THE AUTHOR'S ARGUMENTS:

In this viewpoint Lucille Eleanor Nguyen talks about the American culture of individualism as being one of the ingredients that cause mass shootings. Do you agree? Why or why not?

Having More Guns in America Leads to More Problems in America

"A growing body of data and research shows that owning a gun also increases the risk of a gun-related tragedy."

Center for American Progress

In the following viewpoint, the Center for American Progress exposes the myths surrounding gun ownership. Point by point, the authors argue against myths proposed by the National Rifle Association, which advocates essentially that the more guns people own and use the better and safer it will be for society. As an independent policy institute, the Center for American Progress works to improve the lives of all Americans.

AS YOU READ, CONSIDER THE FOLLOWING QUESTIONS:

1. What is one way that owning a gun puts a person at risk, as stated by the author?
2. According to the viewpoint, why is it rare that a good guy with a gun can stop a bad guy with a gun?
3. Where does most gun violence occur as reported in the viewpoint?

"Myth vs. Fact: Debunking the Gun Lobby's Favorite Talking Points," Center for American Progress, October 5, 2017. Reprinted by permission.

The gun lobby, led by the National Rifle Association (NRA), pursues a number of different policies in state legislatures across the country and in Congress, including eliminating permit requirements for concealed carry; expanding locations where guns may be carried; weakening regulation of the gun industry; and overriding duly enacted state laws that limit gun carrying. While each of these policies have different elements, all are united by a core set of dangerous and misleading arguments perpetuated by the NRA that more guns in more hands will lead to increased personal and community safety.

Below are some of the top NRA-promulgated myths and the facts that expose them as false.

Myth: Owning a gun makes you safer
Fact: Owning a gun puts you at heightened risk for gun violence

The NRA often argues that the United States is a dangerous place and that owning and carrying a gun is the only way to protect both oneself and one's family. While gun ownership is certainly one option for home defense, a growing body of data and research shows that owning a gun also increases the risk of a gun-related tragedy occurring in the home.

- Numerous studies have found that gun ownership increases the risk of both gun-related homicides and suicides.[1]
- Guns in the home are particularly dangerous for victims of domestic violence. The presence of a gun in a home with a history of domestic violence increases the risk that a woman will be killed by 500 percent.[2]
- Guns intended for self-defense are commonly involved in fatal accidents. Studies have shown that across states, higher levels of gun ownership are linked to higher rates of unintentional firearm deaths.[3]

Guns are used far more often in criminal homicides than in justifiable acts of self-defense. In 2014, for every self-defense gun homicide in the United States, guns were used in 34 criminal homicides.[4]

According to some research, the existence of guns leads to more violence and does not effectively increase safety.

Myth: The only thing that stops a bad guy with a gun is a good guy with a gun
Fact: Armed citizens rarely successfully intervene to stop an active shooter

While the NRA actively perpetuates this idea that ensuring a fully armed citizenry is the best approach to stopping so-called bad guys before they are able to do too much damage, there is very little evidence suggesting that civilians can effectively serve this role. Armed citizens often lack training for high-stakes situations and can actually make a bad situation worse. A more effective approach to preventing gun deaths is to enact strong laws and policies to help keep guns out of the wrong hands and limit access to highly dangerous weapons of war.

- An FBI study of 160 active-shooting incidents from 2000 to 2013 found that only one was stopped by an individual with a valid firearms permit. In contrast, 21 incidents were stopped by unarmed citizens.[5]
- Armed citizens can worsen the outcome of a mass shooting. During the 2011 shooting in Tucson, Arizona, an armed bystander misidentified the perpetrator and almost shot the wrong person.[6]
- Expansive concealed carry permitting laws are linked to an increase in violent crime. A 2017 study by researchers at Stanford University found that, 10 years after enacting these laws, states experienced a 13 percent to 15 percent rise in violent crimes.[7]
- Using a gun for defense during a robbery has no significant benefits. A 2015 analysis by researchers at the Harvard T.H. Chan School of Public Health of the National Crime Victimization Survey found that the likelihood of sustaining an injury during a robbery was nearly identical between people who attempted to defend themselves with a gun and those who took no defensive action.[8]
- A gun is more likely to be stolen than used to stop a crime. According to a CAP analysis of the National Crime Victimization Survey, guns are nearly twice as likely to be stolen than to be used for self-defense.[9]

Myth: Mass shooters specifically target gun-free zones
Fact: A small percentage of mass shootings occur in locations where guns are prohibited

This is a corollary to the myth that so-called good guys need to carry guns to protect against prospective shooters. This myth is often used to try to stop legislative efforts to limit gun carrying in certain locations that are considered particularly sensitive or unsuitable for guns, such as schools, houses of worship, or government buildings. However, most of the incidents in the United States in which a single shooter kills four or more people—the FBI's definition of a mass shooting—do not occur in locations where guns are banned but rather in private homes or public locations where individuals are free to carry guns. There is absolutely no evidence that mass shooters specifically seek out locations where guns are banned for acts of mass violence.

- Of the 156 mass shootings that occurred from 2009 to 2016, only 10 percent occurred in so-called "gun-free zones."[10] The majority of these shootings—63 percent—occurred in private homes.[11]

Myth: Gun laws do not work because criminals do not follow the law
Fact: Gun laws are effective at reducing gun violence

The fact that some individuals will undoubtedly violate any given law is not a reason to eliminate such laws altogether. Strong gun laws—such as those requiring background checks for all gun sales; prohibiting certain dangerous people from buying or possessing guns; and limiting access to highly dangerous weapons of war—are effective at helping keep guns out of the wrong hands in order to prevent gun violence and save lives.

- A 2016 CAP study found that the 10 states with the weakest gun laws have an aggregate level of gun violence that is more than three times higher than the 10 states with the strongest gun laws.[12]
- Research by Everytown for Gun Safety found that states that require background checks for all handgun sales have significantly lower rates of intimate partner gun homicides of women; law enforcement officers killed with handguns; and gun-related suicides.[13]

Two studies by the John Hopkins Bloomberg School of Public Health demonstrated the impact of permit-to-purchase laws that include a background check requirement. When Connecticut implemented this law, gun homicides in the state fell 40 percent. When Missouri repealed a similar law, gun homicides in that state rose 25 percent.[14]

Endnotes

1. Matthew Miller and others, "Firearms and Suicide in the United States: Is Risk Independent of Underlying Suicidal Behavior?", American Journal of Epidemiology 178 (6) (2013): 946–955, available at http://aje.oxfordjournals.org/content/early/2013/08/22/aje.kwt197.full.pdf+html; DJ Wiebe, "Homicide and suicide risks associated with firearms in the home: a national case-control study," Annnals of Emergency Medicine 41 (6) (2003): 771–782, available at https://www.ncbi.nlm.nih.gov/pubmed/12764330; LL Dahlberg, RM Ikeda, and MJ Kresnow, "Guns in the home and risk of a violent death in the home: findings from a national study," American Journal of Epidemiology 160 (10) (2004): 929–936, available at https://www.ncbi.nlm.nih.gov/pubmed/15522849; D. Azrael and D. Hemenway, "'In the safety of your own home': results from a national survey on gun use at home," Social Science and Medicine 50 (2) (2000): 285–291, available a https://www.ncbi.nlm.nih.gov/pubmed/10619696.
2. J.C. Campbell and others, "Risk factors for femicide within physically abusive intimate relationships: results from a multi-site case control study," American Journal of Public Health 93 (7) (2003): 1089–1097.
3. Matthew Miller, Deborah Azrael and David Hemenway, "Firearm availability and unintentional firearm deaths, suicide, and homicide among 5-14 year olds," Journal of Trauma and Acute Care Surgery 52 (2) (2002): 274–275, available at https://www.ncbi.nlm.nih.gov/pubmed/11426678.
4. Violence Policy Center, "Firearm Justifiable Homicides and Non-Fatal Self-Defense Gun Use" (2017), available at http://www.vpc.org/studies/justifiable17.pdf.
5. Federal Bureau of Investigation, "A Study of Active Shooter Incidents in the United States Between 2000 and 2013," available at https://www.fbi.gov/news/stories/fbi-releases-study-on-active-shooter-incidents (last accessed October 2017).

6. The Denver Post, "Armed bystander's reaction in Ariz. Shootings illustrates complexity of gun debate," January 15, 2011, available at http://www.denverpost.com/2011/01/15/armed-bystanders-reaction-in-ariz-shootings-illustrates-complexity-of-gun-debate/.

7. John Donohue, Abhay Aneja and Kyle Weber, "Right-to-Carry Laws and Violent Crime: A Comprehensive Assessment Using Panel Data and a State-Level Synthetic Controls Analysis." Working Paper 23510 (The National Bureau of Economic Research 2017), available at http://www.nber.org/papers/w23510.

8. Evan DeFilippis and Devin Hughes, "Gunfight or Flight: New Study Finds No Advantages to Using a Firearm in Self-Defense Situations," The Trace, July 14, 2015, available at https://www.thetrace.org/2015/07/defensive-gun-use-armed-with-reason-hemenway/.

9. Center for American Progress analysis of the National Crime Victimization Survey. While guns were used for self-defense in 85,000 crimes per year from 2010 to 2015, roughly 162,000 guns are stolen each year.

10. Everytown For Gun Safety, "Analysis of Mass Shootings" (2017), available at https://everytownresearch.org/reports/mass-shootings-analysis/

11. Ibid.

12. Chelsea Parsons and Eugenio Weigend, "America Under Fire" (Washington: Center for American Progress, 2016), available at https://www.americanprogress.org/issues/guns-crime/reports/2016/10/11/145830/america-under-fire/.

13. Everytown for Gun Safety, "Background Checks Reduce Gun Violence and Saves Lives" (2015), available at https://everytownresearch.org/wp-content/uploads/2017/01/Background_Check-_FactSheet_web.pdf.

14. Daniel Webster, Cassandra Kercher Crifasi, and Jon S. Vernick, "Effects of the Repeal of Missouri's Handgun Purchaser Licensing Law on Homicides," Journal of Urban Health: Bulletin of the New York Academy of Medicine 91 (3) (2014): 293–302; Daniel Webster, Cassandra Kercher Crifasi, and Jon S. Vernick, "Erratum to: Effects of the Repeal of Missouri's Handgun Purchaser Licensing Law on Homicides," Journal of Urban Health: Bulletin of the New York Academy of Medicine 91 (3) (2014): 598–601.

EVALUATING THE AUTHOR'S ARGUMENTS:

In this viewpoint the Center for American Progress analyzes common myths surrounding guns and gun violence. Choose a side, either for or against owning guns, and construct an argument using points from this viewpoint article.

The Reason a Person Becomes a School Shooter Is Extremely Complex

Sara Martin

"A lot of different factors come together to lead someone to commit an act of mass violence."

In the following viewpoint, Sara Martin interviews well known psychologist Peter Langman to explain why a person might turn to gun violence and commit a school shooting. Martin covers the typical reasons thought to push someone over into extreme violence: bullying, psychopathic or psychotic personalities, stress, trauma, abuse, and other commonly believed causes. Finally, Martin reports on possible prevention. Sara Martin is the editor of the American Psychological Association's online publication, *Monitor on Psychology.*

AS YOU READ, CONSIDER THE FOLLOWING QUESTIONS:
1. As reported by the author, are mass school shootings increasing?
2. Identify two myths about school shooters.
3. Do school shooters have targets? If so who?

WThen the FBI, the U.S. Department of Homeland Security or local police departments want insights on school shooters, they call psychologist Peter Langman, PhD. For over a decade, Langman has conducted research seeking to understand the psychological states and life circumstances of these criminals in an effort to identify the warning signs of impending violence. His website is the world's largest online collection of information on shootings at schools, colleges and universities worldwide, offering information on prevention, threat assessments, school safety and more.

These attacks remain rare: In any given year, the number of mass school shooters is estimated to be one out of 10 million to 20 million people or more, he says. These tragedies are, however, happening more frequently in the United States. While there were three school shootings from 1966 to 1975, that number increased steadily to 19 from 2006 to 2015.

Langman's work has also identified an underappreciated truth: There are no specific symptoms, personal characteristics or conditions associated with someone committing these crimes.

"A lot of different factors come together to lead someone to commit an act of mass violence," says Langman.

What are the most common myths about school shooters?

Perhaps the most important misperception is that school shooters are victims of bullying. Not that that's never true, but its significance has been vastly overblown. Another myth is that mostly juveniles commit these crimes. People in my research are ages 11 to 62, with most of them being adults.

Also, girls can pull a trigger just like boys. Yes, it's less common, but you can't dismiss it as an impossibility. Based on a 50-year review, 95.3 percent of the perpetrators were male and 4.7 percent female.

Another misunderstanding is that school shooters are loners, outsiders who no one talks to. But many school shooters are not isolated. In 2014, for example, a 15-year-old in Washington state, Jaylen Fryberg, became a school shooter a week after he was voted homecoming prince. He was one of the most popular kids in his grade.

Not all victims of bullying open fire on their classmates.

These stereotypes are not only inaccurate but dangerous, because they might lead people to take some threats less seriously than others.

What are the psychological factors associated with school shooters?

Based on my analysis, school shooters typically fall under one of three psychological categories. The first is the psychopathic personality. The second is the psychotic school shooter, who is not fully grounded in reality—they may have schizophrenia or a schizotypal personality disorder. The third category is the traumatized school shooter. These are the people from horrendous family backgrounds who have experienced multiple types of abuse, chronic stress and trauma.

While the psychotic and psychopathic people may have some dysfunction in the home, for the most part, they come from intact, middle-class families. The traumatized shooters are typically from the lower end of the economic spectrum and have parents who are violent, dysfunctional and have criminal histories.

Having said that, I also need to say that most people from those three categories do not commit mass murder. So that's not an explanation, it's a starting point for understanding.

What are the factors that contribute to their committing violence?

Often it's a series of failures, rejections and setbacks. Among adolescents, it could be that a kid gets dumped by his girlfriend around the same time he is suspended from school, around the same time he gets a traffic ticket or gets arrested for something, around the same time he has trouble at home or doesn't make the baseball team—one thing after another. If you take all of that happening to someone who is psychopathic, psychotic or traumatized, then you have some combination of psychological dynamics and life events that put people on a path of violence.

Among adults, their failures are more likely to be failed marriages, occupational failures and—a critical one—financial distress.

Also, with the younger shooters in their 20s and under, they often have some sort of external influence, either a peer recruiting them to join an attack or a "role model." I've found at least a dozen shooters who were drawn to Hitler and the Nazis. It could also be a fictional role model: The movie *Natural Born Killers* has been cited by multiple shooters.

What have you learned about the victims of school shootings?

The popular view is that school shooters are retaliating against tormentors. That's not always true. Out of 48 shooters in my last book

["School Shooters: Understanding High School, College, and Adult Perpetrators," 2015], only one targeted the kid who picked on him.

When a shooter does have a target, most of the time, they are school personnel, teachers and administrators. The next most common targets are female students.

What more can be done to prevent school shootings?

Ideally, all threat-assessment teams in schools and universities should have a psychologist as a member. The primary task for these teams is to investigate threats of violence and separate false alarms from potential or impending violence. Such an investigation can include not only interviewing the person of concern, but also family members, peers, teachers/professors, as well as in some cases obtaining a search warrant to search their homes, rooms and computers. Depending on the situation, the intervention could involve mental health services or a law enforcement intervention such as arrest or detention.

Membership in threat-assessment teams varies within settings. In general, the teams are multidisciplinary, including administration, faculty, law enforcement, mental health and sometimes legal representation. Nothing is simple here, but psychologists are in the best position to interview and evaluate someone, looking for evidence of a psychopathic personality, psychotic issues, and trauma history and to build a relationship with that person to assess them.

> ## EVALUATING THE AUTHOR'S ARGUMENTS:
>
> In this viewpoint Sara Martin presents questions and answers about myths and misunderstandings surrounding school shooters. Did you learn anything you did not previously know or suspect about school shooters? Do you disagree with any findings in the viewpoint?

Violent Video Games Are Not to Blame for School Shootings

Centre for Educational Neuroscience

"Although the link is still debated, and certainly other factors have a bigger influence on aggression, the impact of video games on the behaviour of children and young adults is undeniable."

In the following viewpoint, the Centre for Educational Neuroscience tackles the question of whether violent video games make players more likely to commit acts of violence. The organization provides study-based evidence to back its claims that children and youth who play violent video games are more likely to become aggressive directly after play. However, the authors maintain, connections between playing violent video games and real-life violence have not been established. The Centre for Educational Neuroscience is dedicated to highlighting issues for the education, psychological, and neuroscience disciplines for the benefit of youth.

1. What is the relationship between exposure to violent video games and aggression in children according to the viewpoint?
2. What may result when desensitization occurs after playing violent video games?
3. According to CEN, what positive effect can video games produce?

There is concern among parents, teachers, and society at large, that children who play violent video games, particularly for extended periods of time, might then engage in violent behaviour, or even copy acts of violence experienced during game play. Research to address these concerns is important given that 97% of American teens play video games[1] and children report that they prefer violent to non-violent games[2], so it's unsurprising that there's plenty of studies that look at this issue.

What Questions Should Be Asked?

Researchers need to distinguish correlation from cause. For example, it might be that individuals with greater levels of pre-existing aggression prefer to play more aggressive video games. Here, a correlation would not suggest that the games caused the aggression. By contrast, exposure to aggressive games may be the cause of more aggressive behaviour. Evidence in support of this second possibility would need to use two matched groups, one exposed to the aggressive games, another exposed to some similarly arousing / engaging but not aggressive activity. An increase in aggression should be observed only in the later behaviour of the aggressive game group. Even here, we need to ask, what behaviour will be measured, and how much later should we expect to see the effects—half an hour? The following week?

What's the Evidence?

Not all studies have found a relationship[3] between exposure to violent video games and aggression in children. However, the vast majority of work does show a relationship. In a recent meta-analysis of

While no direct connection has been made, some researchers believe that playing violent video games promotes aggressive behavior in teens.

98 studies, involving 36,965 participants, violent video games were convincingly shown to influence social behaviour[4]. The fact that studies have taken a variety of forms strengthens the certainty of the relationship.

Some work looks at the causal effect of game play by asking some individuals to play violent games in the lab, while others play non-violent games, then measuring the behaviour of each group in social tasks afterwards. These studies have shown that playing violent games results in immediate changes to behaviour[5]. For example, after playing violent games participants are more likely to 'punish' unseen opponents in a task with loud noise bursts, compared to peers who had played a non-violent video game. Young adults also show physiological desensitisation, as measured by less of an increase in heart rate and skin conductance, to scenes of real life violence[6]. Individuals who had played violent, compared with non-violent, games were also less likely to report hearing a fight staged outside the laboratory, judged the fight as less serious, and were slower to respond when they offered help[7]. Desensitisation to violence is thought to link violent game play with later aggressive behaviour[8].

Other studies have considered longitudinal effects, where individuals have been followed over time and video game play at point A has been related to aggression at later point B, both in the lab and also in real life; the more violent play individuals engaged in, the steeper the increase in aggressive behaviour[9].

FAST FACT

According to Pew Research, 60% of adults believe that the amount of gun violence in video games contributes to gun violence in real life.

The size of the effects found in most studies is small to medium, but pretty consistent. As a body of work this indicates that violent games do influence behaviour, rather than just indicating that violent children engage in video games. It's also important to acknowledge however, that although playing violent games does predict both short-term and long-term aggressive behaviour, other factors such as being male and living in poverty have a greater impact on these outcomes[10].

The Effects Vary Across Individuals

The effects of violent games don't seem to be equal for everyone, however. Short-term effects in the laboratory are found to be larger for undergraduate men than women[11], and younger children are more likely to be affected by violent games if they have a high score on the personality trait 'neuroticism' and a low score on the traits 'agreeableness' and 'conscientiousness'[12]. In terms of the game, playing with a personalised avatar has been found to result in more arousal and more aggressive behaviour than when playing with a generic character[13].

The Good News

The good news is that pro-social games, where the main aim is to help someone else, have a positive effect on behaviour[14] to the same extent that violent games have a negative effect. One study asked different groups of participants to play the same game (*Halo II*) but gave them different objectives, with either co-operative or competitive play scenarios. The authors found increased pro-social behaviours only in those playing co-operatively, suggesting that context rather than content might be important[15]. So the power of video games is potentially beneficial for social development. Playing action video games has been used to enhance visual attention and results in faster reaction times[16].

Outstanding Questions

There are still notable questions that have not been adequately considered. Firstly, is there a real-life impact of violent game play on violent crime? The rise seen in video game play over recent decades has not been accompanied by a rise in youth crime rates, and in fact violent crime in youth has fallen over this period. However, there are so many factors that influence crime rates that it would be difficult to pinpoint the effects of any given one. Another major question is whether the same games have a greater impact on the behaviour of younger than older children. How important is it that parents obey the ratings on games? For example, is *Call of Duty* likely to have more of an effect on 14 year olds than on the 18 year olds for whom it is intended? There is currently some evidence that younger children are more effected by violent games than are older children[17], but this is a sorely neglected area of research at the moment.

Take the Rough with the Smooth

Although the link is still debated, and certainly other factors have a bigger influence on aggression, the impact of video games on the behaviour of children and young adults is undeniable both in the short-term and the long-term. Strikingly, one group have noted that the relationship between exposure to violent media and aggressive behaviour is as higher than the link between exposure to lead and IQ scores in children[18].

The potency of video games is an important issue for society, partly because their effects can be negative, but also partly because they can, and could be, positive; indeed it would be difficult to argue for one of these positions without the other. What's vital is that we understand what aspects of games or game play behaviour have an impact, and on whom. The verdict? Although not everyone agrees, the evidence comes down on the side of neuro-hit.

Notes

1. Lenhart, A., Kahne, J., Middaugh, E., Macgill, A. R., Evans, C., & Vitak, J. (2008). Teens, video games, and civics (Report No. 202-415-4500). Washington, DC: Pew Internet and American Life Project.
2. Buchman, D. D., & Funk, J. B. (1996). Video and computer games in the '90s: Children's time commitment and game preference. Children Today, 24, 12-16.
3. Ferguson, C. J., Garza, A., Jerabeck, J., Ramos, R., & Galindo, M. (2013). Not worth the fuss after all? Cross-sectional and prospective data on violent video game influences on aggression, visuospatial cognition and mathematics ability in a sample of youth. Journal of Youth and Adolescence, 42 (1), 109-122. doi: 10.1007/s10964-012-9803-6
4. Greitemeyer, T., & Mügge, D. O. (2014). Video games do affect social outcomes: A meta-analytic review of the effects of violent and prosocial video game play. Personality and Social Psychology Bulletin, 40 (5), 578-589. DOI: 10.1177/0146167213520459
5. Anderson, C. A., Carnagey, N. L., Flanagan, M., Benjamin, A. J., Eubanks, J., & Valentine, J. (2004). Violent video games: Specific effects of violent content on aggressive thoughts and behavior. Advances in Experimental Social Psychology, 36, 199-249.
6. Carnagey, N. L., Anderson, C. A., & Bushman, B. J. (2007). The effect of violence on physiological desensitization to real-life violence. Journal of Experimental Social Psychology, 43 (3), 489-496.
7. Bushman, B. J., & Anderson, C. A. (2009). Comfortably numb: Desensitizing effects of violent media on helping others. Psychological Science, 20, 273–277.
8. Engelhardt, C.R., Bartholow, B.D., Kerr, G.T. & Bushman, B.J. (2011). This is your brain on violent video games: Neural desensitization to violence predicts increased aggression following violent video game exposure, Journal of Experimental Social Psychology, 47 (5), 1033-1036. doi: 10.1016/j.jesp.2011.03.027
9. Willoughby, T., Adachi, P. C., & Good, M. (2012). A longitudinal study of the association between violent video game play and aggression among adolescents. Developmental Psychology, 48, 1044-1057.
10. See Bavalier, D., Green, C. S., & Dye, M. (2010). Children, wired: for better and for worse. Neuron, 67, 692-701.
11. Bartholow, B. D., & Anderson, C. A. (2002). Effects of violent video games on aggressive behaviour: Potential sex differences. Journal of Experimental Social Psychology 38, 283–290 doi:10.1006/jesp.2001.1502
12. Markey, P. M., & Markey, C. N. (2010). Vulnerability to violent video games: A review and integration of personality research. Review of General Psychology, 14 (2), 82-91. DOI: 10.1037/a0019000
13. Fischer, P., Kastenmüller, A., Greitemeyer, T., Media violence and the self: The impact of personalized gaming characters in aggressive video games on aggressive behaviour. (2010). Journal of Experimental Social Psychology, 46 (1), 192-195. doi: 10.1016/j.jesp.2009.06.010
14. Greitemeyer, T., & Osswald, S. (2010). Effects of prosocial video games on prosocial behavior. Journal of Personality and Social Psychology, 98, 211-221.
15. Ewoldsen, D. R., Eno, C. A., Okdie, B. M., Velez, J. A., Guadagno, R. E., & DeCoster, J. (2012). Effect of playing violent video games cooperatively or competitively on subsequent cooperative behaviour. Cyberpsychology, Behavior, and Social Networking, 15 (5), DOI: 10.1089/cyber.2011.0308

16. Dye, M. W. G., Green, C. S., & Bavelier, D. (2009). The development of attention skills in action video game players. Neuropsychologia, 47 (8-9), 1780-1789.doi: 10.1016/j.neuropsychologia.2009.02.002
17. Anderson, C. A., Keio, A. S., Ochanomizu, I., Swing, E. L., Bushman, B. J., Sakamoto, A., Rothstein, H. R., & Saleem, M. (2010). Violent Video Game Effects on Aggression, Empathy, and Prosocial Behavior in Eastern and Western Countries: A Meta-Analytic Review. Psychological Bulletin, 136 (2), 151–173. DOI: 10.1037/a0018251
18. Bushman, B., & Anderson, C. A. (2001). Media violence and the American public.

EVALUATING THE AUTHOR'S ARGUMENTS:

In this viewpoint, the Centre for Educational Neuroscience maintains that playing video games does cause a change in behavior to the player. Using facts from the viewpoint construct an argument to convince someone who doesn't agree.

Violent Media May Aggravate Aggressive Behavior

"The bottom line is that for violent movies and video games, we just do not know the relationship between viewing or playing and aggression in the real world."

Eugene Beresin

In the following viewpoint, Eugene Beresin maintains that there is not a direct causal relationship between violent video games, violent movies, and violent behavior in most young people. The author argues that research studies have not been able to make a link between violent media and violent behavior in the overall population. Beresin contends that a small percentage of youngsters may get into trouble or become violent because of exposure to violent media. Eugene Beresin is a professor of psychiatry at Harvard Medical School and the director of the Child and Adolescent Psychiatry Residency Training Program at Massachusetts General Hospital and McLean Hospital.

AS YOU READ, CONSIDER THE FOLLOWING QUESTIONS:

1. In a study quoted by the viewpoint, why did children play video games?
2. What are the facts about violent movies as reported in the viewpoint?
3. According to the viewpoint, how can parents provide guidance for their children who play video games?

"Research Shows Violent Media Do Not Cause Violent Behavior," by Eugene Beresin, Massachusetts General Hospital, December 26, 2012. Reprinted by permission.

On December 21 the National Rifle Association (NRA) blamed the media for promoting violent video games and movies and then cited these phenomena as the primary causes of mass violence. The assertion that violent video games and movies cause violent behavior has not been demonstrated by scientific research. Youth who have aggressive traits and are stressed are more prone to delinquent and bullying behavior, and are also drawn to these games, but their behavior in real life is not predicted by playing the games. All youth are protected from violence in the world by close, supportive relationships with parents and peers. There are a small percentage of youth, perhaps 5% who are at risk of engaging in violent behavior.

There has been extensive research and writing on the impact of violent movies and videos on behavior in kids. But research is clearly lacking on a direct causal relationship between violent video games and youth violence. Analyses of school shooting incidents from the U.S. Secret Service and the Federal Bureau of Investigation National Center for the Analysis of Violent Crime do not support a link between violent games and real world attacks.

In 2004, a team of Mass General researchers led by Dr. Cheryl Olson studied 1,254 7th and 8th graders and 500 parents in South Carolina and Pennsylvania, looking at what kids were playing, how much time they played, and the possible relationship to delinquent behavior. They found that many of these kids played violent games; two-thirds of 14 year-old boys played at least one violent game often versus a quarter of the girls surveyed. The researchers also found that kids played games to cope with their emotions, to enjoy challenging situations, to keep up with peers playing similar games, to create their own worlds, and to relieve stress.

There were correlations between playing violent games and self-reported physical fights and delinquent behavior, particularly with greater amounts of time played. However, this was only true in a small percentage of children who already exhibited aggressive traits and a high stress level. They found that the traits of aggression and stress were predictive of delinquent behavior and bullying and not the playing of violent video games themselves. Researchers also

Experts believe the effects of media violence on young children can be damaging.

found that parent involvement and parent/peer support seemed to be protective of these negative behaviors.

However, there seems to be a relationship between about five to six percent of kids who get into trouble, sometimes violent, and the amount of time playing violent games. There were no causal relationships found between violent games and violent behavior, just correlations, and this could mean there are other things in life that may be involved.

Problems also exist in the research about violent movies. Most of the science is not very good. However, in the few sound studies, there was also an apparent relationship between the time watching violent TV or movies and aggressive acts in real life—but only for a small percentage of kids and young adults. There seems to be a greater effect on younger children who cannot tell the difference between fantasy and reality. It also appears that when violence is coupled with an attractive movie star and combined with sexuality, the impact appears to be stronger.

The bottom line is that for violent movies and video games, we just do not know the relationship between viewing or playing and aggression in the real world. Research to date does not inform us. But we should be concerned and wary of risks.

Advice for Parents

Here are some tips for parents when they consider their kids video game playing and movie watching:

- Know your kids! If you child is impulsive, aggressive or excessively angry, it may not be wise to allow violent games. If their behavior tends to soften after playing, it may be helping in some manner. By the same token, a fearful, anxious child should refrain from playing games or seeing movies that are filled with horror. Never make your children watch something that they're afraid to watch.

- Sound and supportive relationships with family and peers appear to be protective against violent behavior. Remember that well-adjusted teens are less likely to be at risk.

- Know what your kids are playing and watching. Play the game with your kid to see what the game delivers in terms of content. Watch TV and movies with them and watch for their reaction. For school-age kids and teenagers, use this as an opportunity to talk with them about their reactions to what they see and the impact on them. It is always good to start such discussions early in a child's life, and keep this an ongoing open dialogue.

- Keep an eye on what is developmentally appropriate. Younger kids (or immature children at any age), who cannot tell the difference between reality and fantasy, should not be allowed to watch violent movies, cartoons, or play violent videogames.

- Set guidelines about the amount of time kids can play, and be sure that other activities, such as playing with friends, time with family, etc., provide a good balance.

- Review information about the ratings and content of games at the following sites: Commonsense Media and The Coalition for Quality Children's Media.

EVALUATING THE AUTHOR'S ARGUMENTS:

In this viewpoint Massachusetts General Hospital gives advice to parents on how to guide their children in the area of video game playing. Choose two of the parental tips and analyze how they could make a difference in avoiding violent behavior.

Chapter 3

Is It Possible to Prevent School Shootings?

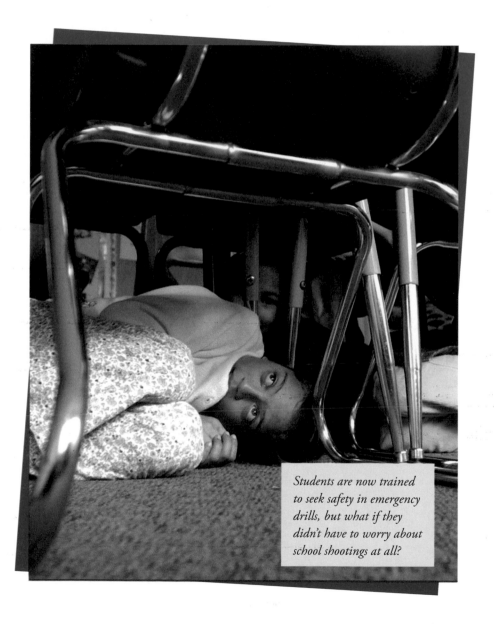

Students are now trained to seek safety in emergency drills, but what if they didn't have to worry about school shootings at all?

Gun Advocates Won't Admit That Guns Are Too Easy to Obtain

"Our current gun laws are riddled with loopholes and allow people to amass enormous arsenals of military-style weapons with virtually no restrictions."

Paul Waldman

In the following viewpoint, Paul Waldman takes offense at gun advocates. Waldman offers a counter to the most common responses to gun control that gun advocates cite after a tragic shooting. In listing the common responses to shootings, the author highlights the fact that gun rights activists say the exact same thing every time—as they did after Columbine, after Sandy Hook, after Parkland—suggesting that things will never change. Paul Waldman is a senior writer and weekly columnist at the *American Prospect*.

AS YOU READ, CONSIDER THE FOLLOWING QUESTIONS:

1. According to Waldman, why don't mass shootings occur in other places besides the United States?
2. What are two ways to thwart shooters as reported in the viewpoint?
3. How do the American people feel about guns as stated in the viewpoint?

There has been yet another mass shooting, something that now seems to occur on a monthly basis. Every time another tragedy like this occurs, gun advocates make the same arguments about why we can't possibly do anything to restrict the weaponization of our culture. Here's a guide to what they'll be saying in the coming days:

1. Now isn't the time to talk about guns.

We're going to hear this over and over, and not just from gun advocates; Jay Carney said it to White House reporters today. But if we're not going to talk about it now, when are we going to talk about it? After Sandy hit the East Coast, no one said, "Now isn't the time to talk about disaster preparedness; best leave that until it doesn't seem so urgent." When there's a terrorist attack, no one says, "Now isn't the time to talk about terrorism." Now is exactly the time.

2. Guns don't kill people, people kill people.

Maybe, but people with guns kill many, many more people than they would if they didn't have guns, and guns designed to kill as many people as possible. We don't know if the murderer in Newtown was suffering from a suicidal depression, but many mass shooters in the past were. And guess what? People suffer from suicidal depression everywhere in the world. People get angry and upset everywhere in the world. But there aren't mass shootings every few weeks in England or Costa Rica or Japan, and the reason is that people in those places who have these impulses don't have an easy way to access lethal weapons and unlimited ammunition. But if you want to kill large numbers of people and you happen to be an American, you'll find it easy to do.

3. If only everybody around was armed, an ordinary civilian could take out a mass killer before he got too far.

If that were true, then how come it never happens? The truth is that in a chaotic situation, even highly trained police officers often kill bystanders. The idea that some accountant who spent a few hours at

Democrats on Capitol Hill have held forums to examine gun violence, its causes, and potential ways to prevent it.

the range would suddenly turn into Jason Bourne and take out the killer without doing more harm than good has no basis in reality.

4. We don't need more laws, we just need to enforce the laws we have.

The people who say this are the same ones who fight to make sure that existing laws are as weak and ineffectual as possible. Our current gun laws are riddled with loopholes and allow people to amass enormous arsenals of military-style weapons with virtually no restrictions.

5. Criminals will always find a way to get guns no matter what measures we take, so what's the point?

The question isn't whether we could snap our fingers and make every gun disappear. It's whether we can make it harder for criminals to get guns, and harder for an unbalanced person with murderous intent to kill so many people. The goal is to reduce violence as much as possible. There's no other problem for which we'd say if we can't solve it completely and forever we shouldn't even try.

6. The Constitution says I have a right to own guns.

Yes it does, but for some reason gun advocates think that the right to bear arms is the only constitutional right that is virtually without limit. You have the right to practice your religion, but not if your religion involves human sacrifice. You have the right to free speech, but you can still be prosecuted for incitement or conspiracy, and you can be sued for libel. Every right is subject to limitation when it begins to threaten others, and the Supreme Court has affirmed that even though there is an individual right to gun ownership, the government can put reasonable restrictions on that right.

And we all know that if this shooter turns out to have a Muslim name, plenty of Americans, including plenty of gun owners, will be more than happy to give up all kinds of rights in the name of fighting terrorism. Have the government read my email? Have my cell phone company turn over my call records? Check which books I'm taking out of the library? Make me take my shoes off before getting on a plane, just because some idiot tried to blow up his sneakers? Sure, do what you've got to do. But don't make it harder to buy thousands of rounds of ammunition, because if we couldn't do that we'd no longer be free.

7. Widespread gun ownership is a guarantee against tyranny.

If that had anything to do with contemporary life, then mature democracies would be constantly overthrown by despots. But they aren't. We shouldn't write laws based on the fantasies of conspiracy theorists.

8. Guns are a part of American culture.

Indeed they are, but so are a lot of things, and that tells us nothing about whether they're good or bad and how we want to treat them going forward. Slavery was a part of American culture for a couple of hundred years, but eventually we decided it had to go.

9. The American people don't want more gun control.

The truth is that when public opinion polls have asked Americans about specific measures, the public is in favor of a much more restrictive gun regime than we have now. Significant majorities would like to see the assault weapons ban reinstated, mandatory licensing and training for all gun owners, significant waiting periods for purchases, and host of other restrictions (there are more details here). In many cases, gun owners themselves support more restrictions than we currently have.

10. Having movie theaters and schools full of kids periodically shot up is just a price we should be willing to pay if it means I get to play with guns and pretend I'm Wyatt Earp.

OK, that's actually an argument gun advocates don't make. But it's the truth that lies beneath all their other arguments. All that we suffer because of the proliferation of guns—these horrifying tragedies, the 30,000 Americans who are killed every year with guns—for gun advocates, it's unfortunate, but it's a price they're willing to pay. If only they'd have the guts to say it.

EVALUATING THE AUTHOR'S ARGUMENTS:

In this viewpoint Paul Waldman argues against the common complaints of gun enthusiasts. Compare and contrast Waldman's points with those from the Center for American Progress in Chapter 2.

Arming Teachers Not Much of a Solution

> "An armed guard or armed staff on school grounds can reduce the number of casualties in a mass shooting situation by up to 70 percent."

Creighton Suter

In the following viewpoint Creighton Suter of the *Purdue Exponent* explores the proposed solution of arming teachers and administrators. When district budgets don't allow armed guards on site, or when those guards fail to do their job, as was the case in the Marjory Stoneman Douglas High School tragedy, teachers could be an important line of defense against school shooters. Suter cites experts who approach the problem from an engineering perspective, focusing on how to stop shooters before they can do damage. Still, the author asserts, many teachers are uncomfortable with the idea of being armed and taking on the responsibility of killing or injuring another human. The viewpoint suggests that finding a solution to this societal problem should come from evidence-based reasoning rather than emotional response.

"Research Shows Armed Teachers Could Reduce Casualties," by Creighton Suter, Purdue Exponent, March 1, 2018. Reprinted by permission, purdueexponent.org.

AS YOU READ, CONSIDER THE FOLLOWING QUESTIONS:
1. As reported by Suter, what controversial suggestion has been made by President Trump concerning school shooters?
2. According to research studies, could armed teachers be effective in saving lives during school shooting incidents?
3. As stated by the author, what should be done instead of arming teachers?

Nationally, the average response time of police is 10 minutes. In an active shooter situation—like the one seen at Marjory Stoneman Douglas High School in Parkland, Florida, just a few weeks ago—each second it takes for first responders to arrive on scene can mean life or death for victims.

A controversial plan to limit the loss of life in such an instance was given fuel recently when President Donald Trump endorsed it, igniting a national debate on its validity. The proposal suggests teachers and school administrators—who are willing to do so—arm themselves to provide yet another option of last resort if confronted with a shooter.

The proposal has drawn criticism from teachers and gun control advocates alike; however, a Purdue professor and homeland security expert has conducted research that supports the plan's premise.

Professor Eric Dietz, previously the executive director for the Indiana Department of Homeland Security, conducted research in 2014 that found having either an armed guard or armed staff on school grounds can reduce the number of casualties in a mass shooting situation by up to 70 percent by, at the very least, slowing an attacker.

"Time is your ally," he said.

In an ideal scenario, Dietz said, a campus would have multiple school resource officers, who are usually trained police officers, on or near the school grounds. MSDS in Parkland had such a safety measure in place, but that officer failed to enter the building after being made aware of the shooting for reasons that are still unclear.

Both the Lafayette and West Lafayette Police Departments have trained school resource officers on staff.

Some parents are so concerned about school shootings that they have made the decision to homeschool their children.

After tragedies like the one at MSDS or Sandy Hook Elementary School in 2012, advocates on both side of the gun debate come out in force.

"There's a mass of people that come out and say no guns," Dietz said. "Then you have the people that favor guns coming out and saying, 'Well it's not the guns. … It's the one person who was disturbed that did the killing.'"

Many of the arguments, both for and against the proposal to arm teachers, are grounded in emotion. Dietz's research, on the other hand, approaches the topic from an engineering perspective.

"What we were trying to do is offer some insight to the trade-offs and value judgements to treat the school safety problem," he said.

If trained resource officers are not available because of budgetary constraints or other considerations, armed teachers or administrators can have a similar effect, according to Dietz's research. Having as few as 5 to 10 percent of a school's staff armed with a firearm could reduce casualties by 5 to 20 percent, his research showed.

Professor Janet Alsup, head of the College of Education's department of curriculum and instruction has reservations about the proposal.

"I think it's very problematic," she said in an email. "Teachers are educated to be experts in pedagogy, learning sciences, and their content areas,

not in armed combat. If we begin to require (or even strongly suggest) that teachers in k-12 classrooms should be willing and able to engage in armed confrontations with school shooters, this puts an undue burden on individual teachers—and on the profession at large."

Before coming to Purdue, Alsup spent time as a middle and high school teacher. Even if she was given the opportunity as a teacher, she said she would not have considered carrying a firearm.

"I think it would have undermined my role and impact considerably," she said. "It would have changed both how I thought about my job as teacher and how I understood others' expectations of me."

Dietz said that he would never suggest someone who has any apprehension about carrying a weapon to do so. In fact, he said those are the last people he would like to see carrying a firearm.

The Indiana State Teachers Association released a statement that called on legislators to provide more resources to aid students struggling with trauma rather than bring weapons into a learning environment.

"Arming educators sends a signal that we are giving up and accepting this crisis as the new reality," the statement read. "Instead of arming educators with guns, lawmakers should start by arming our schools with more psychologists and counselors so kids dealing with trauma get care before they become broken. Educators need to be focused on teaching our students. Together—parents, educators, lawmakers, community leaders—need to come up with real solutions that really will save lives."

No matter which side of the debate one falls on, the goal is the same: save lives.

"Every life is precious," Dietz said.

But Dietz urged legislators to use evidence-based reasoning when deciding how best to address the pressing issue.

"After these big events, we want to do things that have been shown to have a deliberate impact on reducing casualties, not something we hope, suspect or have faith will reduce casualties."

EVALUATING THE AUTHOR'S ARGUMENTS:

In this viewpoint Creighton Suter reports that some researchers are in favor of arming teachers while others are not. How did the author use interviews to make a case for or against arming teachers?

Parents, Schools, and Communities Can Prevent School Shootings

"Communities also help raise children. With many eyes and ears, they can detect often smaller problems before young people grow into violence."

Elizabeth Englander

In the following viewpoint, Elizabeth Englander contends that to prevent school shootings a team consisting of parents, schools, and communities should work together instead of waiting for the government to take action. Englander provides specific instructions in what she believes can address potential threats of young people, such as mental health, isolation, and aggression. Elizabeth Englander directs the Massachusetts Aggression Reduction Center and is a professor of psychology.

AS YOU READ, CONSIDER THE FOLLOWING QUESTIONS:

1. How can schools prevent violence according to Englander?
2. What suggestions does Englander offer to social media companies so they could help?
3. What should parents do according to the viewpoint article?

"10 Ways Schools, Parents and Communities Can Prevent School Shootings Now," by Elizabeth Englander, The Conversation, February 16, 2018. https://theconversation.com/10-ways-schools-parents-and-communities-can-prevent-school-shootings-now-91960. Licensed Under CC BY-ND 4.0 International.

After a shooter killed 17 people at a Florida high school, many have expressed frustration at the political hand-wringing over gun control and calls for prayer.

As a parent, I understand the desire for practical responses to school shootings. I also absolutely believe the government should do more to prevent such incidents. But the gun control debate has proven so divisive and ineffective that I am weary of waiting for politicians to act.

I study the kind of aggressive childhood behavior that often predates school shootings. That research suggests what communities and families can start doing today to better protect children. Here are 10 actions we can all take while the federal government drags its heels.

What Schools Can Do

Because educators observe students' emotional and behavioral development daily, they are best positioned to detect troubled behaviors and intervene. In Los Angeles, for example, schools have successfully used outreach and training to identify potentially violent students before problems occur.

Teach Social and Emotional Skills

Children learn social skills from everyday interactions with each other. Playtime teaches young people how to control their emotions, recognize others' feelings and to negotiate. Neighborhood "kick the can" games, for example, require cooperation to have fun – all without adult supervision.

Today, frequent social media use and a decrease in free play time has reduced children's opportunities to learn these basic social skills.

But social and emotional skills can—and should—be taught in school as a way to prevent student violence. Students with more fluent social skills connect better with others and may be more able to recognize troubled peers who need help.

Hire More Counselors and School Resource Officers

Due to budget cuts, many schools have few or no trained school psychologists, social workers or adjustment counselors on staff. These mental health professionals are society's first line of defense against

Parents, teachers, and others in the community can help prevent school shootings by supporting the social and emotional development of kids.

troubled students—specially with the current increase in adolescent depression and anxiety.

In my opinion, school resource officers—trained police officers who work with children—are also helpful for students. While untrained officers may pose a threat to students, well-trained school resource officers can connect with kids who have few other relationships, acting as a support system. They are also on hand to respond quickly if crime or violence erupts.

Is It Possible to Prevent School Shootings? 91

Putting trained school resource officers and counselors in every school will cost money, but I believe it will save lives.

Use Technology to Identify Troubled Students

Technology may challenge kids' social development, but it can also be harnessed for good. Anonymous reporting systems – perhaps text-message based—can make it easier for parents and students to alert law enforcement and school counselors to kids who seem disconnected or disturbed. That enables early intervention.

In Steamboat Springs, Colorado, one such tip appeared to prevent extreme violence in May 2017. Police took a young man who'd threatened to harm his peers into protective custody before he could act on his words.

What Communities Can Do

Communities also help raise children. With many eyes and ears, they can detect often smaller problems before young people grow into violence.

Doctors Should Conduct Standard Mental Health Screenings

Extreme violence is almost always preceded by certain behavioral problems. These typically include a propensity toward aggression, a marked lack of social connectedness, indications of serious mental illness and a fascination with violence and guns.

Doctors could detect these problems early on with a standardized screening at health checkups. If concerns arise, referrals to counseling or other mental health professionals might follow.

Enlist Social Media Companies in the Effort to Detect Threats

Most young people today use social media to express their feelings and aspirations. In the case of school shooters, these posts are often violent. A single violent post is hardly a guarantee of homicidal acts, of course. But evidence strongly indicates that repeated expressions of this nature can be a sign of trouble.

I would like to see companies like Instagram, Twitter and Snapchat create algorithms that identify repeated online threats and automatically alert local law enforcement.

What Parents Can Do

Parents and guardians are often the first to detect their child's emotional struggles. Here are some tips for monitoring and promoting healthy emotional development at home.

Think Critically About Your Child's Social Media Use

From virtual war games to cruel trolls, the internet is full of violence. The relationship between violent content and aggression hasn't been consistent in research: Some studies see no relationship at all, while others find some correlation between violent video games and violent behavior.

This mixed evidence suggests that online content affects children differently, so parents must assess how well their child handles it. If your daughter likes "Assassin's Creed" but is gentle, socially successful and happy, the onscreen violence may not be strongly impacting her.

But if your child is drawn to violent games and tends to be aggressive or troubled, discuss the situation with your pediatrician or school counselor.

Consider What Your Child Is Missing Out On

Is your child sleeping properly? Do your kids socialize with other young people? These two behaviors are linked to mental health in children, and excessive screen time can reduce or diminish the quality of both.

Make sure digital devices aren't disrupting your kids' sleep, and schedule play dates if your kids don't make plans on their own.

Assess Your Child's Relationships

Like adults, children need confidants to feel invested in and connected with their community. The trusted person can be parent, a family member or a friend—just make sure someone's playing that role.

For children who struggle to make friends and build relationships, there are programs that can help them learn how.

Fret Productively About Screen Time

Research shows that excessive screen time can damage kids' brains. That's alarming in part because parents can't realistically keep kids entirely off devices.

So rather than just fret over screen time, focus instead on how children can benefit from a variety of activities. Evidence shows that children who experience different pursuits over the course of their day—from sports and music to an after-school job—are happier and healthier for it.

Talk with Your Child

This is both the easiest and hardest way to make sure your kids are doing OK. Children, especially teenagers, don't always want to talk about how life is going. Ask anyway.

My research shows that simply asking children about their friends, their technology use and their day is an important way to show you care. Even if they don't respond, your interest demonstrates that you're there for them.

Try this one now. Ask your children what they're thinking about the shooting in Florida and how they like their friends and school. Then listen.

EVALUATING THE AUTHOR'S ARGUMENTS:

In this viewpoint Elizabeth Englander presents an effective way to potentially prevent school shootings. Englander presents specific ways that parents, schools, and community members can help youth. How does the author's perspective differ from most others in this resource?

Enhanced Security Won't Stop School Shootings

"Overall there is little empirical evidence that such security measures decrease the likelihood of school shootings."

Bryan Warnick, Benjamin A. Johnson, and Sam Rocha

In the following viewpoint, Bryan Warnick, Benjamin A. Johnson, and Sam Rocha argue that enhancing school security systems won't prevent school shootings. The authors contend that these enhanced systems could even backfire and cause more incidents of violence. Warnick outlines ways that he believes schools should change their culture instead of relying on security. Bryan Warnick is a professor of education at Ohio State University. Benjamin A. Johnson is a professor in Utah Valley University's department of student leadership and success studies. Sam Rocha is a professor of education at the University of British Columbia.

AS YOU READ, CONSIDER THE FOLLOWING QUESTIONS:
1. As stated in the viewpoint, what is "target-hardening?"
2. According to the authors, why do security measures backfire?
3. What is one issue presented in the viewpoint that might possibly cause violence in an individual?

When deadly school shootings like the one that took place on Valentine's Day in Broward County, Florida occur, often they are followed by calls for more stringent security measures.

For instance, after the Jan. 23 case in which a 15-year-old student allegedly shot and killed two students and wounded 16 others at a small-town high school in Kentucky, some Kentucky lawmakers called for armed teachers and staff.

If anything, the response of the Kentucky lawmakers represents what has been called the "target-hardening" approach to school shootings. This approach attempts to fortify schools against gun violence through increased security measures. These measures may include metal detectors, lock-down policies, "run, hide, fight" training and surveillance cameras.

While some of these measures seem sensible, overall there is little empirical evidence that such security measures decrease the likelihood of school shootings. Surveillance cameras were powerless to stop the carnage in Columbine and school lock-down policies did not save the children at Sandy Hook.

As researchers who have collaboratively written about school shootings, we believe what is missing from the discussion is the idea of an educational response. Current policy responses do not address the fundamental question of why so many mass shootings take place in schools. To answer this question, we need to get to the heart of how students experience school and the meaning that schools have in American life.

An educational response is important because the "target hardening" approach might actually make things worse by changing students' experience of schools in ways that suggest violence rather than prevent it.

How Security Measures Can Backfire

Filling schools with metal detectors, surveillance cameras, police officers and gun-wielding teachers tells students that schools are scary, dangerous and violent places—places where violence is expected to occur.

Preventative security measures, such as metal detectors and school security guards, often are ineffective or worse.

The "target hardening" approach also has the potential to change how teachers, students and administrators see one another. How teachers understand the children and youth they teach has important educational consequences. Are students budding citizens or future workers? Are they plants to nourish or clay to mold?

One of the most common recommendations for schools, for example, is that they should be engaged in threat assessment. Checklists are sometimes suggested to school personnel to determine when students should be considered as having the potential for harm. While such practices have their place, as a society we should be aware that these practices change how teachers think of students: not as budding learners, but potential shooters; not with the potential to grow and flourish, but with the potential to enact lethal harm.

Of course, society can think of students in different ways at different times. But the more teachers think of students as threats to be assessed, the less educators will think of students as individuals to nourish and cultivate.

As researchers, we have read the accounts of dozens of different school shootings, and we think educators, parents and others should begin to raise the following questions about schools.

Questions of Status

To what extent does the school—through things like athletics, homecoming royalties, or dances and so forth—encourage what some political scientists have called the "status tournament of adolescence" that lurks behind the stories of many school shootings?

As one reads about such shootings, one often senses a feeling of social anxiety and betrayal on the part of perpetrator. Americans hold high expectations for schools as places of friendship and romance, yet too often students find alienation, humiliation and isolation. The frustration at these thwarted expectations at least sometimes seems to turn toward the school itself.

Force and Control Issues

To what extent does the force and coercion employed by many schools contribute to a "might makes right" mentality and associated violence?

It is true that bullying is part of some of the stories of school shooters. Students who are bullied or who are bullies themselves will quite naturally think of schools as places appropriate for violence. There is also sometimes a rage, however, against the day-to-day imposition of school discipline and punishment. Since schools are experienced as places of force and control, for some students, they also come to be seen as appropriate places for violence.

Identity and Expression

In research on American high schools, one finds the idea that American schools are intertwined with notions of "expressive individualism"—the idea that human beings should find out and be true to who they really are on the inside. Might this also contribute to school shootings?

Suburban high schools, in particular, are seen by the middle class as places to accomplish expressive projects. Sociologist Robert Bulman points out, for example, how Hollywood films set in suburban settings focus on student journeys of self-discovery, while urban school films focus on heroic teachers and academic achievement. In the same vein, many suburban school shooters see what they are doing as acts of self-expression.

Reading stories of school shootings, one often finds moments in which the shooters claim that something inside, whether hatred or frustration, needed to find expression. An example of this is the manifesto left by Luke Woodham, who shot two students in 1997. "I am not spoiled or lazy," he wrote, "for murder is not weak or slow-witted, murder is gutsy and daring." The school became the place where Woodham thought he could express the gutsy and daring person he found on the inside.

What to Do

Of course, it will be difficult to definitively answer the questions we have posed above. And, even if we are able to find answers, it is not clear what the proper educational response should be.

For example, self-expression might be a valuable task for schools, even if it is found to contribute in some way to school shootings. Our suggestion is simply that, instead of trying to find solutions to school shootings in the dubious arms of security technologies, or even solely through more promising public policy, society should ask deeper questions about the nature of education and schooling in American society.

It is time to think about school shootings not as a problem of security, but also as a problem of education.

> **EVALUATING THE AUTHORS' ARGUMENTS:**
>
> The viewpoint authors argue that for a variety of reasons enhanced school security won't work to prevent school shootings. Do the authors suggest alternatives that might work instead? Is it enough to identify a problem in order to make a solid argument, or should the authors propose a better solution?

Arming Teachers Is the Best Option

Brittany Elena Morris

"At least the students and staff won't be sitting ducks if a maniac comes into the school."

In the following viewpoint, Brittany Elena Morris reports on a bill proposed by the Arizona House of Representatives in 2014. The bill would allow deadly weapons on school grounds, provided those in possession were properly trained and certified. Proponents of the bill argue that, when resources don't allow for security officers, teachers are the next line of defense. Brittany Elena Morris is a graduate of the Walter Cronkite School of Journalism and Mass Communication and is an assignment editor for NBC News.

AS YOU READ, CONSIDER THE FOLLOWING QUESTIONS:
1. What did HB2412, the School Safety Designee Program, propose?
2. Why would rural schools benefit more from arming teachers?
3. What arguments do critics of the house bill make, according to the viewpoint?

Giving trained schoolteachers and staff access to firearms in storage lockers is a way to secure campuses when it isn't possible to provide resource officers, a state lawmaker contends.

"The danger in our schools is an issue that isn't going to go away unless we do something about it," said Rep. David Stevens, R-Sierra Vista. "Arming our teachers is the best option at this point."

Stevens authored HB 2412, which would allow a person to possess a deadly weapon on school grounds if he or she has completed training outlined in the bill and has been designated to do so by a school district or charter school governing board. Dubbed the School Safety Designee Program, it would be optional for public or private schools.

It's currently against state law to have a firearm on a school campus unless the person is a law enforcement officer or has special permission.

The bill won an endorsement Feb. 26 from the House Appropriations Committee, with all three Democrats present voting against it. It was awaiting action on the House floor.

Stevens noted that the National Rifle Association proposed the idea in response to tragedies such as those at Sandy Hook Elementary School in Newtown, Conn., as a less-expensive alternative to putting resource officers in every school. He said a similar bill he introduced last year failed because it wouldn't have provided special training.

Attorney General Tom Horne, who proposed the change in Arizona, called the program a "golden mean" between allowing teachers to carry firearms and hiring resource officers for all schools.

"At least the students and staff won't be sitting ducks if a maniac comes into the school," he said.

Stevens noted that the Sierra Vista Unified School District has three resource officers for six elementary schools as well as its middle school and high school campuses. One officer is at Buena High School every day, while the others travel among schools as needed.

"If something bad happened, how long would it take for the officer to get there?" Stevens said. "If a teacher is trained with a firearm, they will be quicker to respond."

Should teachers be trained and armed to act as a first line of defense for their students?

Candidates would receive training on how to clean, handle and store firearms, would take courses in marksmanship, judgmental shooting and other subjects and would be conditioned on how to use deadly force. They would have to repeat the training every year.

The Attorney General's Office would establish the standards for candidates and oversee certification.

The firearms would have to be stored in secure lockers and could only be removed from school grounds for training, cleaning and maintenance.

Both the Arizona School Board Association and the Arizona Education Association, the state's largest teachers union, registered as opposed to the bill. While neither organization explained its position to the committee, Horne said the Arizona School Boards Association indicated that it might support a bill applying only to rural schools a certain distance from the nearest police station.

Kent Scribner, superintendent of the Phoenix Union High School District, said in an interview that he opposes introducing more guns on campus.

"Trained and sworn officers should be the only ones ensuring our security," said Scribner, who oversees more 27,000 students on 16 campuses.

The district recently held a community forum on safety after shots were fired outside Cesar Chavez High School during an evening basketball game. No one was hurt or arrested.

Elgin Nelson, whose son attends Betty H. Fairfax High School, was at the forum. He said the last thing his neighborhood or the state needs is more access to guns.

"They allow this Wild, Wild West," Nelson said. "It's particularly irresponsible on the part of our state Legislature."

Rep. Andrew Sherwood, D-Tempe, who voted against the bill, said his office was inundated with calls from concerned community members.

"I am frustrated because I think we can do better," Sherwood said. "There is no proof guns in schools make it safer. We were elected to create jobs, but instead we are talking about guns again."

Reps. Stefanie Mach, D-Tucson, and Lela Alston, D-Phoenix, also voted against the bill.

Rep. John Kavanagh, R-Fountain Hills, chairman of the House Appropriations Committee, said the bill is a defense against maniacs.

"I have no doubt this bill is going to help Arizona and will pass," he said. "A lot of kids are going to die if there isn't someone in that school to protect them."

EVALUATING THE AUTHOR'S ARGUMENTS:

In this viewpoint Brittany Elena Morris reports on the Arizona state legislation supporting the arming of school employees. Based on the perspectives quoted in the viewpoint, how would you feel if your teachers were armed?

Arming Teachers Is a Preposterous Idea

"Asking teachers to learn how to use weapons while teaching is downright dangerous."

Marcie Craig

In the following viewpoint Marcie Craig joins the debate surrounding the issue of arming classroom teachers to fix the violence in schools. Craig reports on ways states are effectively saying "no" to armed classroom teachers. The author cites reasons against the arming of teachers and argues that teaching literacy is challenging enough without adding the burden of being responsible for security. Marcie Craig is the director of the International Literacy Association.

AS YOU READ, CONSIDER THE FOLLOWING QUESTIONS:

1. According to Craig, what are some states doing to prevent arming classroom teachers?
2. Why are teaching and security different as stated by the author?
3. What does the International Literacy Association suggest doing about school violence?

"Arming Teachers Is Not a Solution to Stop Gun Violence in Schools," by Marcie Craig, International Literacy Association, March 7, 2018. Reprinted by permission.

The prevalence of school shootings in the United States underscores an urgent and, so far, unmet need of devising comprehensive measures that protect students, teachers, and staff in education spaces.

While the specifics of those measures are, and ought to be, open to fair debate, the notion that arming teachers is the best answer to preventing recurrences of this type of tragedy is preposterous.

We are already seeing action. State lawmakers across the country have introduced legislation specifically prohibiting classroom teachers from carry guns, such as in New York. And, earlier this week, the Florida state Senate took action to halt the movement toward arming classroom educators.

Teaching and security enforcement are two different roles. Combining them is impractical and unwise, even if proposed with the best of intentions. The challenges of effective literacy instruction for students are formidable enough. Neither teachers, nor students, should have to wrestle with the distraction of gun-equipped classrooms.

Everyone deserves to feel safe in the classroom. Teachers need to give their full attention and effort to each day's learning. They need schools unfettered by violence. What we are hearing from our members and other educators is that introducing weapons into the teacher-student relationship shatters any shared sense of safety and security.

Talk to literacy teachers and you will quickly find out how precious a commodity their instructional time is, and how demanding a preparation is required for them to be at their most effective in the classroom. Asking teachers to learn how to use weapons, arm themselves, and undertake security enforcement roles while teaching is not only burdensome, distracting, and education-impairing, it's downright dangerous.

To place on teachers the additional responsibility of having to use deadly physical force against an armed assailant who has managed to enter school grounds with lethal ordinance distorts and perverts the teaching function. It further puts teachers and students at risk as shown by instances where weapons have accidently or, at times intentionally, been misused.

Many teachers want to focus on educating and nurturing students, not using a weapon against them. Should teachers be required to use a firearm if necessary?

It also gives would-be assailants the ultimate and undeserved victory of making schools a weapons-based environment.

This is hardly the legacy that teachers and students at schools which have had to contend with episodes of gun violence would wish for. We owe it to them and to ourselves to do much better than that.

The International Literacy Association denounces the very idea of arming classroom teachers. Yes, we should talk about how we can increase safety of school perimeters. Yes, we should talk about resources to help early identification and treatment for mental health issues. And yes, we need better communication and coordination between the agencies we have in place to protect us.

That's why ILA calls upon government officials, federal and local authorities, and school officials to fashion security measures for the nation's schools that preserve safe learning spaces by keeping the instruments of violence out of them, save for those possessed by law enforcement officers.

Many commentators on the Marjory Stoneman Douglas High School tragedy have noted the maturity and eloquence of the school's students whom they have spoken with on the air. The students are indeed striking examples of the poignancy and power that literacy education instills.

We're proud of these students and proud of their teachers. We want to see a solution for school security that supports without diminishing the focused learning opportunities they have enjoyed and leveraged to such an impressive effect.

EVALUATING THE AUTHOR'S ARGUMENTS:

In this viewpoint Marcie Craig argues that arming classroom teachers is absolutely not a good idea. What makes this author's perspective different than others you've read in this resource? Does that make her argument more or less persuasive?

Facts About School Shootings

Editor's note: These facts can be used in reports to add credibility when making important points or claims.

Risks in Life:

- Children do not risk their lives attending school (mass school shootings are rare events).
- An American's chance of dying in some mass shooting=1 in 11,125.
- An American's chance of dying in a car accident=1 in 491.
- An American's chance of drowning=1 in 1,133.
- An American's chance of choking on food=1 in 3,461.
- About 30,000 Americans die from firearms in a year (this includes all types not just school shootings).
- About 20–30 mass murders or shootings occur in the United States each year. On average once per year at a school.
- About 55 million children attend school in the United States. On average over the past 25 years, about 10 students were killed per year by gunfire at school.

Shooting Statistics
Since 1996

- 8 mass shootings (killing at least 4 people) at K-12 schools in the United States.
- 16 multiple victim shootings (4 or more victims, at least 2 deaths) in schools.

Past 25 years

- An average of one mass murder (killing of four or more by any means) in an American school each year.

Daily

- 96 Americans are killed by guns.

Most Deadly School Shootings in US History:
   University of Texas in 1996
   Columbine High School in 1999
   Virginia Tech School in 2007
   Sandy Hook Elementary School in 2012
   Parkland, Florida, High School in 2018

Arming Teachers:

- 59% of Americans oppose and 41% favor the idea.

Gun Statistics in America:

- 50% of Americans say that gun violence is a very big problem.
- 53% of Americans say it is too easy to get illegal guns (this causes the problem).
- 47% of Americans say there would be fewer mass shootings if it was harder to get legal guns.
- 33% of Americans say there would be less crime if more people owned guns.
- 35% of Americans say there would be more crime if more people owned guns.

Gun Ownership in America:

- 42% of Americans live in households where there are guns.
- 57% of Americans live in households with no guns.
- 2/3 of gun owning Americans cite protection as the reason for ownership.
- 4 in 10 of gun owning Americans cite hunting as the reason for ownership.

Gun Law Statistics:

- About 68% of Americans support stricter gun laws.
- About 25% of Americans oppose stricter gun laws.
- 81% of Americans want a minimum age limit of 21 to buy guns.
- 81% of Americans want a 3 day waiting period to purchase guns.
- 88% of Americans want required background checks of anyone buying a gun.

Organizations to Contact

The editors have compiled the following list of organizations concerned with the issues debated in this book. The descriptions are derived from materials provided by the organizations. All have publications or information available for interested readers. The list was compiled on the date of publication of the present volume; the information provided here may change. Be aware that many organizations take several weeks or longer to respond to inquiries, so allow as much time as possible for the receipt of requested materials.

The Brady Campaign to Prevent Gun Violence
840 First Street NE, Suite 400
Washington, DC. 20002
Phone: (202) 370-8100
Email: Use contact page
Website: http://www.bradycampaign.org/
The Brady Campaign to Prevent Gun Violence is a national organization with a bold mission: to cut gun deaths in the United States in half by 2025. This website has a broad amount of information about guns and gun violence in the United States. Four times a year, the organization publishes a newsletter, the *Brady Report*. Past and present issues are available online.

CATO Institute
1000 Massachusetts Avenue
NW, Washington, DC 20001-5403
Phone: (202) 842-0200
Email: Use contact page
Website: www.cato.org
The CATO Institute is a research organization. They specialize in providing clear and thoughtful information on public policy issues. CATO uses a variety of venues including blogs, web features, TV, and others to get their points across.

Center for American Progress
1333 H Street NW, 10th Floor
Washington, DC 20005
Phone: (202) 682-1611
Website: www.americanprogress.org/about/contact-us/
The Center for American Progress is a nonpartisan institute that dedicates its actions to improving the lives of Americans. They want to shape the national debate on many issues including gun violence and security. The center has strong coverage on gun violence prevention.

Center for Educational Neuroscience
University College London
Website: http://www.educationalneuroscience.org.uk/
The Center for Educational Neuroscience is a group of researchers from two colleges and an educational institute working together combining the disciplines of psychology, neuroscience, and education. The center has resources for community members and teachers, and it specializes in analyzing and giving insight into problem behaviors of children.

Everytown for Gun Safety Support Fund
450 Lexington Avenue, New York, NY 10022
Phone: (646) 324-8250
Email: info@everytown.org
Website: https://everytownresearch.org/
Everytown for Gun Safety Support Fund is an independent, nonpartisan organization dedicated to understanding gun violence in the United States. This group works toward a goal of education and reduction of armed violence. They actively address issues of guns and gun violence through an extensive website with online fact sheets, infographic, maps, reports, and other documents.

Federal Bureau of Investigation (FBI)
935 Pennsylvania Avenue NW
Washington, DC. 20535-0001
Phone: (202) 324-3000
Email: Contact local FBI headquarters via email listed for each state.

Website: https://www.fbi.gov/
The Federal Bureau of Investigation is a national security agency of the United States. This agency is dedicated to protecting citizens, communities, and businesses from threats of all kinds. The FBI investigates all types of crime, and their website contains a vast range of information on such items.

Giffords Law Center to Prevent Gun Violence
268 Bush Street #555
San Francisco, CA, 94104
Phone: (415) 433-2062
Email: lawcenter@giffords.org
Website: https://lawcenter.giffords.org/
The Giffords Law Center to Prevent Gun Violence is an organization of legal experts working to research, write, and promote laws and practices that are proven to save lives from gun violence. The center's mission is one of active participation through workshops, representation, outreach, and education. Their website contains a wealth of resources about gun laws and other aspects of gun violence.

The Heritage Foundation
214 Massachusetts Avenue NE
Washington, DC. 20002-4999
Phone: (202) 546-4400
Email: info@heritage.org
Website: https://www.heritage.org/
The Heritage Foundation is a conservatively based research and educational institution. Their mission is to fight for traditional American values including free enterprise, limited government, individual freedom, and a strong national defense. The foundation's website includes informative commentary on the issues surrounding gun violence.

For Further Information

Books

Doeden, Matt. *Gun Control: Prevention Violence or Crushing Constitutional Rights?* Minneapolis,MN: Twenty-First Century Books, 2012.

Dissects the contentious issue of guns and gun control. Considers points made by gun control advocates and gun enthusiasts.

Fast, Jonathan. *Ceremonial Violence: A Psychological Explanation of School Shootings.* New York,NY: Overlook Press, 2008.

Provides information about Columbine High School and four other school shootings. Looks at abnormal psychology and why teens commit school rampage violence.

Hogg, David. *#Never Again: A New Generation Draws the Line.* New York,NY: Random House, 2018.

Two survivors of the Parkland, Florida, school shooting deliver a powerful message. They inform readers about the movement #NeverAgain to stop gun violence.

Klebold, Sue. *A Mother's Reckoning: Living in the Aftermath of Tragedy.* New York,NY: Crown, 2016.

Mother of one of the shooters at Columbine uses personal recollections to write about her son's case. She tries to come to terms with her son's crime and hopes to help other families recognize warning signs of possible problems.

Klein, Jessie. *The Bully Society: School Shootings and the Crisis of Bullying in America's Schools.* New York,NY: New York University Press, 2012.

Analyzes the topic of bullying. Includes information about different types of bullying.

Lysiak, Matthew. *Newtown: An American Tragedy.* New York,NY: Gallery Books, 2013.

Investigates the Sandy Hook school shooting in Newtown, Connecticut. Delves into the development of the shooter from young boy to school shooter.

MacKay, Jenny. *The Columbine School Shootings.* Farmington Hills,MI: Gale Cengage Learning, 2010.

Discusses the Columbine school shooting in Colorado. Focuses on the crime itself and the response to the emergency.

Merino, Noel. *Gun Violence.* Farmington Hills,MI: Greenhaven Press, 2015.

In a debate style of pros and cons, takes a look at gun violence. Whether gun violence is a serious problem, what contributes to it, and what can be done to reduce the problem.

Nakaya, Andrea C. *Thinking Critically: Mass Shootings.* San Diego,CA: Reference Point Press, 2015.

Examines issues related to mass shootings. Examines whether violent video games play a part, if stricter gun control laws would help, and mental health issues.

Periodicals and Internet Sources

Alter, Charlotte, "The Young and the Relentless," *Time*, March 22, 2018. http://time.com/magazine/us/5210502/april-2nd-2018-vol-191-no-12-u-s/.

Blad, Evie, "Do Schools' 'Active-Shooter' Drills Prepare of Frighten?" Education Week, September 19, 2017. https://www.edweek.org/ew/articles/2017/09/20/do-schools-active-shooter-drills-prepare-or-frighten.html.

Cooke, Charles C. W., "The Truth About the Second Amendment," *National Review*, August 9, 2018. https://www.nationalreview.com/magazine/2018/08/27/the-truth-about-the-second-amendment/.

Deprez, Esme E., "Guns in America," *Bloomberg*, February 23, 2018. https://www.bloomberg.com/quicktake/americans-and-their-guns.

Dreher, Beth, "How to Keep Our Kids Safe in School As the Gun Debate Rages On," *Woman's Day*, September 25, 2018. https://www.womansday.com/life/real-women/a22996676/school-shooting-survivors-safety-ideas/.

Epps, Garrett, "The Second Amendment Does Not Transcend All Others," *Atlantic*, March 8, 2018. https://www.theatlantic.com/politics/archive/2018/03/second-amendment-text-context/555101/.

Hoffner, Lori A., "Ready to Respond Versus React," National Recreation and Park Association, August 1, 2018. https://www.nrpa.org/parks-recreation-magazine/2018/august/ready-to-respond-versus-react/.

Lithwick, Dahlia, "The March for Our Lives Activists Who Said Never Again," *Glamour*, November 1, 2018. https://www.glamour.com/story/women-of-the-year-2018-march-for-our-lives-activists.

Newman, Alex, "'March for Our Lives' Lies," *New American*, April 11, 2018. https://www.thenewamerican.com/print-magazine/item/28699-march-for-our-lives-lies.

Olson, Tod, "Can Teens Change the World," Scholastic Action, September 2018. https://action.scholastic.com/issues/2018-19/090118/can-teens-change-the-world.html#670L.

Shapiro, Amy, "Columbine Principal Reflects on 'Worst Nightmare' 19 Years After Shooting," ABC News, April 19, 2018. https://abcnews.go.com/US/columbine-principal-reflects-worst-nightmare-19-years-shooting/story?id=54540073.

Shusterman, Noah, "What the Second Amendment Really Meant to the Founders," *Washington Post*, February 22, 2018. https://www.washingtonpost.com/news/made-by-history/wp/2018/02/22/what-the-second-amendment-really-meant-to-the-founders/?utm_term=.286229666193.

Smith, Patricia, "Why We're Still Arguing About Gun Control," *New York Times* Upfront, November 20, 2017. https://upfront.scholastic.com/issues/2017-18/112017/why-we-re-still-arguing-about-gun-control.html#1170L.

Truesdell, Jeff, "Grief and Outrage: After a Gunman Kills 17 in a Florida School," *People*, February 21, 2018. https://people.com/crime/florida-school-shooting-grief-outrage/.

Tzintzun, Cristina, "Texas Millennials Move the Needle," *Dissent*, Summer 2018. https://www.dissentmagazine.org/article/texas-millennials-move-needle-latino-organizing.

Williamsen, Kurt, "Getting Rid of Guns," *New American*, April 10, 2018. https://www.thenewamerican.com/print-magazine/item/28701-getting-rid-of-guns.

Witt, Emily, "How the Survivors of Parkland Began the Never Again

Movement," *New Yorker*, February 19, 2018. https://www.newyorker.com/news/news-desk/how-the-survivors-of-parkland-began-the-never-again-movement.

Zornick, George, "The Adults Have Failed, So Students Are Leading the Way," *Nation*, March 24, 2018. https://www.thenation.com/article/the-adults-have-failed-so-students-are-leading-the-way/.

Websites

Factcheck.org (https://www.factcheck.org/2015/10/gun-laws-deaths-and-crimes/)
This website presents arguments from President Barack Obama and former presidential candidate Carly Fiorina. They debate gun laws, deaths, and crimes.

Federal Bureau of Investigation (FBI) (https://www.fbi.gov/)
The FBI's website contains a large repository of information about school shootings.

National Center for Health Statistics (https://www.cdc.gov/nchs/pressroom/sosmap/Firearm.htm)
This is a website of the national Centers for Disease Control and Prevention (CDC). This page presents a graphic displaying data on how many deaths by firearms per state occurred in 2014.

National Constitution Center (https://constitutioncenter.org)
This nonpartisan American institution was established by Congress to provide accurate information about the Constitution of the United States. Check out the interactive website, including the Second Amendment: The Right to Bear Arms.

National Institute of Justice (https://www.nij.gov/topics/crime/school-crime/Pages/welcome.aspx)
Find a variety of school safety information at this site. Check out the School Safety Initiative, a program related to bullying and school safety.

Index

Picture Credits

Cover Joe Raedle/Getty Images; p. 10 Michele Eve Sandberg/AFP/Getty Images; p. 13 Daniel M Ernst/Shutterstock.com; p.18 Saul Loeb/AFP/Getty Images; p. 23 Monkey Business Images/Shutterstock.com; p. 29 © iStockphoto.com/monkeybusinessimages; p. 34 Michael Candelori/Shutterstock.com; p. 39 Rawpixel.com/Shutterstock.com; p. 42 mooremedia/Shutterstock.com; p. 45 Julie Dermansky/Corbis News/Getty Images; p. 51 AFP/Getty Images; p. 56 Jeff Greenberg/Universal Images/Getty Images; p. 63 Daisy Daisy/Shutterstock.com; p. 68 Andrey_Popov/Shutterstock.com; p. 75 © iStockphoto.com/klebercordeiro; p. 78 ZUMA Press, Inc./Alamy Stock Photo; p. 81 SIPA/AP Images; pp. 86, 97 © AP Images; p. 91 SpeedKingz/Shutterstock.com; p. 102 Syda Productions/Shutterstock.com; p. 106 Giles Clarke/Getty Images.